SUBTRACTION

Twin 248CD
718451024826
ISBN-10: 1-57583-893-1
ISBN-13: 978-157583-893-9

Credits:

Publisher: Twin Sisters Productions, LLC
Executive Producers: Kim Mitzo Thompson, Karen Mitzo Hilderbrand
Music By: Kim Mitzo Thompson, Karen Mitzo Hilderbrand, Hal Wright
Music Arranged By: Hal Wright
Workbook Authors: Kim Mitzo Thompson, Karen Mitzo Hilderbrand, Ken Carder
Book Design: Steven Dewitt

www.twinsisters.com   1-800-248-TWIN(8946)

Table of Contents

How to Use This Subtraction Music CD and Workbook

Music makes learning fun and easy! We're confident that the songs and activities included in this 96-page Workbook and Music CD set will make learning subtraction a bit easier...and definitely a bit more fun.

The original songs teach each fact 0 through 18 and several strategies that help many students better understand the concept of subtraction. The lyrics to the songs are included in this book. Encourage your child to listen to the music CD each day for a week or longer. Listen together in the car!

This workbook features explanations, practice worksheets, learning games and challenges that can be played alone or with a partner—or even an entire classroom! Make photocopies of the pages for repeated practice. Many activities use the 20-sided dice that you can cut out and assemble in minutes.

Children should have addition, subtraction, multiplication and division facts at their fingertips before they leave elementary school. For some, memorization comes easy. For others, memorization is much more difficult. In all cases, memorization must follow an understanding of the concept. Look for ways to count, combine, and sort objects. Look, too, for patterns and reasoning or strategies that help your child understand subtraction.

Listen and learn the songs together. Complete the worksheets and play the games together. Above all, enjoy the time together.

Words You Should Know:

SUBTRACTION: An operation that takes some away from another.

MINUEND: The quantity from which you're subtracting.

SUBTRAHEND: The number you are subtracting from the MINUEND

DIFFERENCE: The answer in subtraction; the result of subtracting a SUBTRAHEND from a MINUEND.

MINUS SIGN: – The symbol in a number sentence that tells you that you are supposed to subtract. When you read 3 – 2 you say, "Three minus two."

EQUAL SIGN: = The symbol in a number sentence that tells you that the numbers on either side have the same value. In 3 – 2 = 1, the number 1 has the same value as 3 – 2.

REGROUPING: To name a number in a different way. For example, 25 is the same as two tens and five ones. Some call this RENAMING or BORROWING.

#1 There's No Doubt About It

There's no doubt. There's no doubt.
There's no doubt. There's no doubt.

There's no doubt about it–the answer stays the same.
There's no doubt about it–the answer will remain.
For when you are subtracting, and a zero you see,
to figure out the answer is so easy!

Chorus
Stay on that number–don't make a move.
Stay on that number–there's none to remove.
Stay on that number–for the answer, you see,
is the same number. It's so easy!

1 – 0 is 1	2 – 0 is 2	3 – 0 is 3
4 – 0 is 4	5 – 0 is 5	6 – 0 is 6
7 – 0 is 7	8 – 0 is 8	9 – 0 is 9

(**Chorus**)

10 – 0 is 10	11 – 0 is 11	12 – 0 is 12
13 – 0 is 13	14 – 0 is 14	15 – 0 is 15
16 – 0 is 16	17 – 0 is 17	18 – 0 is 18

There's no doubt about it–the answer stays the same.
There's no doubt about it–the answer will remain.
For when you are subtracting, and a zero you see,
to figure out the answer is so easy!

(**Chorus**)

There's no doubt (there's no doubt).
There's no doubt (no, not one).
There's no doubt (the answer remains).
There's no doubt (it stays the same).

$$1-0=1$$
$$2-0=2$$
$$3-0=3$$
$$4-0=4$$

Zero "0" Strategy

When you're subtracting zero, don't make a move.
Stay on the number– then there's none to remove.

1 - 0 is 1	Think, "I have 1 and none to remove."
2 - 0 is 2	Think, "I have 2 and none to remove."
3 - 0 is 3	Think, "I have 3 and none to remove."
4 - 0 is 4	Think, "I have 4 and none to remove."
5 - 0 is 5	Think, "I have 5 and none to remove."
6 - 0 is 6	Think, "I have 6 and none to remove."
7 - 0 is 7	Think, "I have 7 and none to remove."
8 - 0 is 8	Think, "I have 8 and none to remove."
9 - 0 is 9	Think, "I have 9 and none to remove."

Now, you do it!

10 – 0 is ____ Think, "I have ____ and ____ to remove."

11 – 0 is ____ Think, "I have ____ and ____ to remove."

12 – 0 is ____ Think, "I have ____ and ____ to remove."

13 – 0 is ____ Think, "I have ____ and ____ to remove."

14 – 0 is ____ Think, "I have ____ and ____ to remove."

15 – 0 is ____ Think, "I have ____ and ____ to remove."

16 – 0 is ____ Think, "I have ____ and ____ to remove."

17 – 0 is ____ Think, "I have ____ and ____ to remove."

18 – 0 is ____ Think, "I have ____ and ____ to remove."

#2 The Answer Is Zero Every Time

Chorus
The answer is zero every time.
The answer is zero–this is not a line.
The answer is zero–yes, it's true.
Any number minus itself is always zero–
this is a subtraction rule!

1 – 1 is 0	2 – 2 is 0	3 – 3 is 0
4 – 4 is 0	5 – 5 is 0	6 – 6 is 0
7 – 7 is 0	8 – 8 is 0	9 – 9 is 0

(Chorus)

10 – 10 is 0	11 – 11 is 0
12 – 12 is 0	13 – 13 is 0

Okay, I think you have it.
Any number minus itself is always zero.

It doesn't matter if it's 10 or 15 or even 1,033.
The rule's the same. It really is true.
This is a subtraction rule.
Any number minus itself is always zero.

The answer is zero every time.
The answer is zero–this is not a line.
The answer is zero–yes, it's true.
This is a subtraction rule!

Sames Strategy

When you subtract any number from the same number, the answer is always "0."

1 - 1 is 0   Think, "I start with 1. I take away 1. That leaves me none!"

2 - 2 is 0   Think, "I start with 2. I take away 2. That leaves me none!"

3 - 3 is 0   Think, "I start with 3. I take away 3. That leaves me none!"

4 - 4 is 0   Think, "I start with 4. I take away 4. That leaves me none!"

5 - 5 is 0   Think, "I start with 5. I take away 5. That leaves me none!"

6 - 6 is 0   Think, "I start with 6. I take away 6. That leaves me none!"

7 - 7 is 0   Think, "I start with 7. I take away 7. That leaves me none!"

8 - 8 is 0   Think, "I start with 8. I take away 8. That leaves me none!"

9 - 9 is 0   Think, "I start with 9. I take away 9. That leaves me none!"

✳ The SAMES STRATEGY works with any number!

10 - 10 is _____ Think, "I start with ___. I take away ___. That leaves me _____."

18 - 18 is _____ Think, "I start with ___. I take away ___. That leaves me _____."

58 - 58 is _____ Think, "I start with ___. I take away ___. That leaves me _____."

191 - 191 is _____ Think, "I start with ___. I take away ___. That leaves me _____."

265 - 265 is _____ Think, "I start with ___. I take away ___. That leaves me _____."

547 - 547 is _____ Think, "I start with ___. I take away ___. That leaves me _____."

1,033 – 1,033 is _____ Think, "I start with ___. I take away ___. That leaves me _____."

#3 Just Count Down One

COUNTDOWN STRATEGY:
If you're subtracting one, just count down one!

1 - 1 is 0. Think, *1. Count down one. 0!*

2 - 1 is 1. Think, *2. Count down one. 1!*

3 - 1 is 2. Think, *3. Count down one. 2!*

4 - 1 is 3. Think, *4. Count down one. 3!*

5 - 1 is 4. Think, *5. Count down one. 4!*

6 - 1 is 5. Think, *6. Count down one. 5!*

7 - 1 is 6. Think, *7. Count down one. 6*

The COUNTDOWN STRATEGY works with any number!

8 – 1 is _____. Think, _____. *Count down one._____.*

12 – 1 is _____. Think, _____. *Count down one._____.*

26 – 1 is _____. Think, _____. *Count down one._____.*

53 – 1 is _____. Think, _____. *Count down one._____.*

101 – 1 is _____. Think, _____. *Count down one._____.*

595 – 1 is _____. Think, _____. *Count down one._____.*

1,065 – 1 is _____. Think, _____. *Count down one._____.*

Write the number that is one less. Subtract.

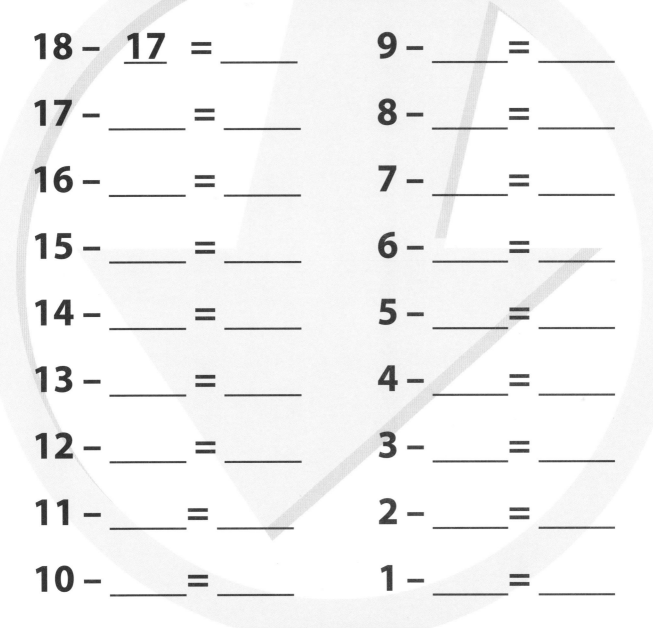

18 – _17_ = _____   9 – _____ = _____

17 – _____ = _____   8 – _____ = _____

16 – _____ = _____   7 – _____ = _____

15 – _____ = _____   6 – _____ = _____

14 – _____ = _____   5 – _____ = _____

13 – _____ = _____   4 – _____ = _____

12 – _____ = _____   3 – _____ = _____

11 – _____ = _____   2 – _____ = _____

10 – _____ = _____   1 – _____ = _____

What pattern do you see?

_____

_____

_____

-0, -1, Same Number

1	2	3	4	5	6	7	8	9	10
- 0	- 0	- 0	- 0	- 0	- 0	- 0	- 0	- 0	- 0

11	12	13	14	15	16	17	18	1	2
- 0	- 0	- 0	- 0	- 0	- 0	- 0	- 0	- 1	- 2

3	4	5	6	7	8	9	10	11	12
- 3	- 4	- 5	- 6	- 7	- 8	- 9	- 10	- 11	- 12

13	14	15	16	17	18	1	2	3	4
- 13	- 14	- 15	- 16	- 17	- 18	- 1	- 1	- 1	- 1

5	6	7	8	9	10	11	12	13	14
- 1	- 1	- 1	- 1	- 1	- 1	- 1	- 1	- 1	- 1

15	16	17	18	14	6	7	12	5	9
- 1	- 1	- 1	- 1	- 0	- 6	- 1	- 12	- 1	- 0

10

Race a partner through the maze! Roll one 20-sided die. Subtract 0, 1, or the same number from the number rolled. Move your marker to the next space that matches that difference. The first player to reach the exit with a zero is the winner.

START	END								
1	**0**	2	4	6	8	11	1	4	15
14	2	8	1	2	14	15	12	17	16
10	13	3	7	3	17	13	16	13	3
11	9	12	4	6	7	18	19	9	12
4	16	9	11	5	5	10	9	11	17
14	3	15	20	10	6	18	20	4	11
18	12	5	14	6	20	15	19	8	16
8	2	19	7	1	5	8	18	2	7
17	16	3	19	11	20	4	7	9	1
6	8	10	4	6	17	3	15	19	10
15	1	9	11	5	20	18	4	20	5
10	13	7	14	12	16	2	14	9	13
12	14	19	1	15	13	8	18	2	6

#4

Take It Away!

Take it!

Take it away. I'm talkin' subtract.
Take it away. You can do the math.

Take it away. *Minus* is the word.
Take it away. For it's time to learn.

Chorus
Take it, take it, take it, take it, take it–
take it away.
Take it, take it, take it, take it, take it–
I'll lead the way.

Take it, take it, take it, take it, take it–
facts up to five.
Take it, take it, take it, take it, take it–
I'll be your guide.

> **TIP:** When you are subtracting 1, 2, 3, or 4 from a number, begin with the top number and count down the bottom number of times. For example, for the problem 10 - 4, think, *10, 9, 8, 7, 6.* *6 is the answer.*

Ones! 1 – 1 is 0
Twos! 2 – 1 is 1   2 – 2 is 0
Threes!   3 – 1 is 2   3 – 2 is 1   3 – 3 is 0

(Chorus)

Fours!   4 – 1 is 3   4 – 2 is 2   4 – 3 is 1   4 – 4 is 0
Fives!   5 – 1 is 4   5 – 2 is 3   5 – 3 is 2   5 – 4 is 1   5 – 5 is 0

(Chorus)

Take it away. I'm talkin' subtract.
Take it away. You can do the math.

Take it away. *Minus* is the word.
Take it away, for it's time to learn.

(Subtrus 2x)

Take it!

Minuends 1, 2, 3, 4, 5

1	2	2	3	3	3	4	4	4	4
- 1	- 1	- 2	- 1	- 2	- 3	- 1	- 2	- 3	- 4

5	5	5	5	5	2	5	4	1	3
- 1	- 2	- 3	- 4	- 5	- 2	- 1	- 3	- 1	- 1

5	4	5	3	2	3	5	2	4	5
- 5	- 2	- 1	- 3	- 1	- 2	- 4	- 2	- 3	- 3

2	4	5	3	2	3	5	2	5	3
- 2	- 1	- 5	- 2	- 1	- 1	- 3	- 1	- 4	- 3

1	2	4	3	2	5	4	3	4	5
- 1	- 2	- 2	- 1	- 2	- 2	- 4	- 2	- 3	- 5

2	5	3	5	4	1	4	5	3	2
- 1	- 5	- 3	- 1	- 1	- 1	- 2	- 4	- 2	- 2

#5

Sound Off

Sound off! (Sound off!)
Let's go! (Let's go!)
Left, left, left, right, left. (Left, left, left, right, left.)

Chorus
We're going to learn our subtraction facts.
(We're going to learn our subtraction facts.)
We'll say them loud, as a matter of fact.
(We'll say them loud, as a matter of fact.)
When I say the facts out loud,
(When I say the facts out loud,)
answer me–and sound proud.
(answer me–and sound proud.)

Let's start with the facts of six.
(Let's start with the facts of six.)
Shout the answer. Please be quick.
(Shout the answer. Please be quick.)

6 – 1 equals 5   6 – 2 equals 4
        6 – 3 equals 3

This is fun. Don't you agree?
(This is fun. Don't you agree?)

6 – 4 equals 2   6 – 5 equals 1
        6 – 6 equals 0

You're a real subtraction hero.
(You're a real subtraction hero.)

(Chorus)

The facts of seven are next in line.
(The facts of seven are next in line.)
Keep the beat and steady time.
(Keep the beat and steady time.)

7 – 1 equals 6   7 – 2 equals 5
        7 – 3 equals 4

Are you ready for some more?
(Are you ready for some more?)

7 – 4 equals 3   7 – 5 equals 2
7 – 6 equals 1   7 – 7 equals 0

You're a real subtraction hero.
(You're a real subtraction hero.)

We just learned our subtraction facts.
(We just learned our subtraction facts.)
The 6s and 7s, as a matter of fact.
(The 6s and 7s, as a matter of fact.)

We said them loud. We said them clear.
(We said them loud. We said them clear.)
And now it's time for a great big cheer.
(And now it's time for a great big cheer.)

Minuends 1, 2, 3, 4, 5

1	2	2	3	3	3	4	4	4	4
- 1	- 1	- 2	- 1	- 2	- 3	- 1	- 2	- 3	- 4

5	5	5	5	5	2	5	4	1	3
- 1	- 2	- 3	- 4	- 5	- 2	- 1	- 3	- 1	- 1

5	4	5	3	2	3	5	2	4	5
- 5	- 2	- 1	- 3	- 1	- 2	- 4	- 2	- 3	- 3

2	4	5	3	2	3	5	2	5	3
- 2	- 1	- 5	- 2	- 1	- 1	- 3	- 1	- 4	- 3

1	2	4	3	2	5	4	3	4	5
- 1	- 2	- 2	- 1	- 2	- 2	- 4	- 2	- 3	- 5

2	5	3	5	4	1	4	5	3	2
- 1	- 5	- 3	- 1	- 1	- 1	- 2	- 4	- 2	- 2

Minuends 1, 2, 3, 4, 5

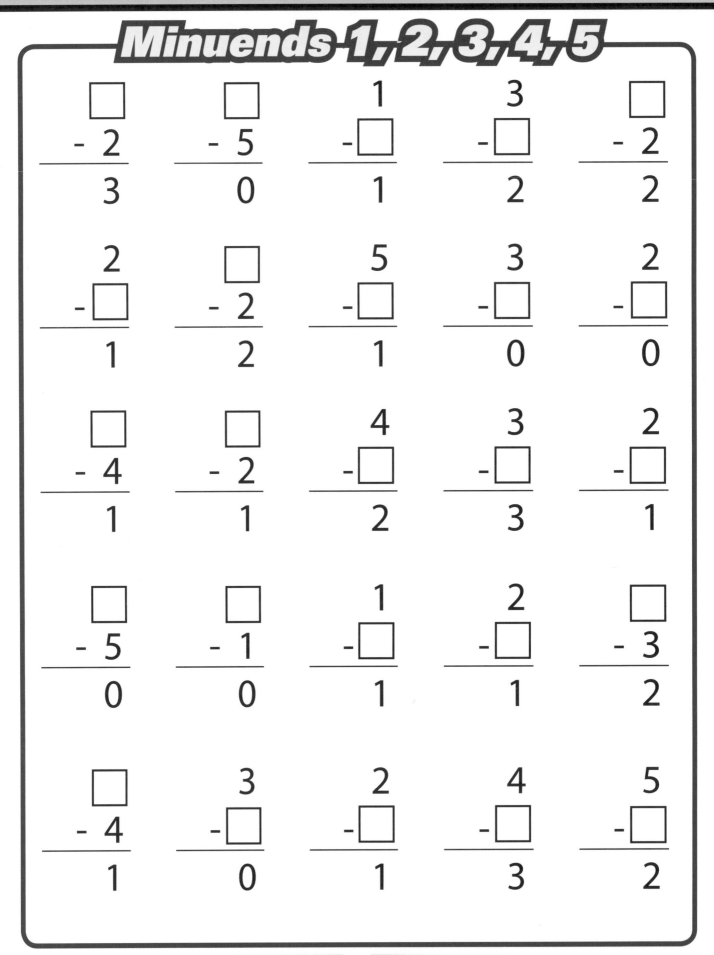

☐	☐	1	3	☐
− 2	− 5	− ☐	− ☐	− 2
3	0	1	2	2

2	☐	5	3	2
− ☐	− 2	− ☐	− ☐	− ☐
1	2	1	0	0

☐	☐	4	3	2
− 4	− 2	− ☐	− ☐	− ☐
1	1	2	3	1

☐	☐	1	2	☐
− 5	− 1	− ☐	− ☐	− 3
0	0	1	1	2

☐	3	2	4	5
− 4	− ☐	− ☐	− ☐	− ☐
1	0	1	3	2

14

1	2	2	3	3
− 1	− 1	− 2	− 1	− 2

3	4	4	4	4
− 3	− 1	− 2	− 3	− 4

5	5	5	5	5
− 1	− 2	− 3	− 4	− 5

Problem Search

Subtract and write the **difference**.
Find and circle the subtraction
facts in the puzzle.

3	-	1	=	2	1	-	0	5	2
-	5	-	5	=	0	4	3	1	-
3	-	2	=	1	1	-	4	-	1
=	5	=	0	4	4	5	=	1	=
4	1	-	4	-	3	-	3	=	1
-	5	2	=	3	-	3	=	0	2
4	5	-	2	=	3	=	-	1	3
-	3	2	-	1	-	5	=	5	=
4	-	=	3	-	=	-	2	-	4
=	-	0	4	5	1	3	5	4	3
0	0	=	4	-	1	=	3	=	1
5	-	1	=	4	-	2	3	1	=
2	4	-	2	=	2	5	=	2	3

Sound Off

Sound off! (Sound off!)
Let's go! (Let's go!)
Left, left, left, right, left. (Left, left, left, right, left.)

Chorus
We're going to learn our subtraction facts.
(We're going to learn our subtraction facts.)
We'll say them loud, as a matter of fact.
(We'll say them loud, as a matter of fact.)
When I say the facts out loud,
(When I say the facts out loud,)
answer me–and sound proud.
(answer me–and sound proud.)

Let's start with the facts of six.
(Let's start with the facts of six.)
Shout the answer. Please be quick.
(Shout the answer. Please be quick.)

6 – 1 equals 5   6 – 2 equals 4
        6 – 3 equals 3

This is fun. Don't you agree?
(This is fun. Don't you agree?)

6 – 4 equals 2   6 – 5 equals 1
        6 – 6 equals 0

You're a real subtraction hero.
(You're a real subtraction hero.)

(Chorus)

The facts of seven are next in line.
(The facts of seven are next in line.)
Keep the beat and steady time.
(Keep the beat and steady time.)

7 – 1 equals 6   7 – 2 equals 5
        7 – 3 equals 4

Are you ready for some more?
(Are you ready for some more?)

7 – 4 equals 3   7 – 5 equals 2
7 – 6 equals 1   7 – 7 equals 0

You're a real subtraction hero.
(You're a real subtraction hero.)

We just learned our subtraction facts.
(We just learned our subtraction facts.)
The 6s and 7s, as a matter of fact.
(The 6s and 7s, as a matter of fact.)

We said them loud. We said them clear.
(We said them loud. We said them clear.)
And now it's time for a great big cheer.
(And now it's time for a great big cheer.)

Minuends 6, 7

6 - 0	6 - 1	6 - 2	6 - 3	6 - 4	6 - 5	6 - 6	7 - 0	7 - 1	7 - 2
7 - 3	7 - 4	7 - 5	7 - 6	7 - 7	6 - 2	6 - 6	7 - 1	7 - 3	6 - 2
6 - 0	7 - 1	7 - 2	6 - 3	6 - 4	7 - 5	6 - 6	6 - 0	7 - 7	6 - 2
7 - 0	6 - 1	6 - 2	7 - 3	7 - 4	6 - 5	7 - 6	6 - 0	6 - 1	7 - 2
7 - 5	6 - 4	6 - 1	7 - 7	6 - 5	6 - 2	6 - 6	7 - 3	7 - 6	6 - 3
6 - 1	6 - 6	6 - 2	7 - 3	7 - 4	7 - 5	6 - 5	7 - 0	7 - 2	6 - 6

Fill In The Missing Number

Fill in the missing numbers to make a subtraction fact of 6 or 7.
Circle the subtraction facts. The facts may be found horizontally and vertically.

5	3	7	-	4	=		2	1	8
9	7	-	3	=	6	-		=	0
7	-		=	7	10	3	-	8	
-	6	=	7	-		=	2	7	-
	-	6	=		4	3	=		2
=	6	-		=	2	5		-	=
0	1	5	11		-	3	=		5
8	10	=	12	8			-	0	=	6
6	-		=	5	4	2	9	4	10

$$
\begin{array}{ccccc}
6 & 6 & 6 & 6 & 6 \\
-\,0 & -\,1 & -\,2 & -\,3 & -\,4 \\
\end{array}
$$

$$
\begin{array}{ccccc}
7 & 6 & 6 & 7 & 7 \\
-\,7 & -\,5 & -\,6 & -\,0 & -\,1 \\
\end{array}
$$

$$
\begin{array}{ccccc}
7 & 7 & 7 & 7 & 7 \\
-\,2 & -\,3 & -\,4 & -\,5 & -\,6 \\
\end{array}
$$

Race To The Center

Practice the subtraction facts 0 – 7. Say each subtraction sentence and the difference. Predict how quickly you can move to the center. Set a timer and discover how well you know subtraction facts!

6-0	7-1	6-3	4-1	3-3	2-2	7-2	5-3	4-2	3-1
7-4	5-3	4-4	1-0	4-1	7-6	5-1	6-4	5-2	7-7
5-2	4-3	5-1	6-6	7-5	3-2	4-0	3-1	2-1	6-5
7-3	4-2	7-5	7-7	2-1	5-2	5-5	7-6	4-3	4-2
1-1	6-3	2-1	2-2	6-2	★	6-4	7-1	5-0	4-3
4-2	3-3	6-4	7-5	4-1	7-7	6-5	2-1	4-2	5-5
6-0	5-1	5-2	6-4	7-1	6-5	2-2	5-3	2-1	4-3
7-7	3-2	5-2	6-2	3-1	5-3	4-2	7-4	7-2	5-4
4-3	7-0	6-5	4-2	5-5	6-3	3-1	4-3	5-2	6-4
6-2	5-3	4-3	5-2	7-1	7-5	4-1	3-2	1-1	1-0
5-0	6-4	7-3	5-5	3-1	2-2	1-0	6-6	5-2	7-5
4-2	5-2	7-0	5-3	5-1	6-3	7-6	6-0	4-2	2-1

Think Addition

I know that we're learning subtraction facts.
I know that we're learning "take-away" math.
I know that we're trying to be exact,
but I need you to concentrate when you subtract.

Chorus
Think *addition*. Think *addition*.
It's easy to *subtract* if you think *addition*.

When you are solving a problem
and you need to subtract,
I want you to think *addition facts*.

If you know your addition facts, it will help you
When you subtract. Let's look at the problem 8 - 5.
I want you to think, *5 and what make 8*? If you
know that 5 + 3 = 8, then this strategy will help you
solve your subtraction facts! The "think addition"
approach will work with all of your subtraction facts.
It's a great strategy.

Let us practice this concept with our facts of 8.
Let us think *addition* as the answer we'll state.
I will say the problem. Just follow my lead.
It's the only way to learn, don't you agree?

8 - 1... Think, *1 and what make 8?* (7) 8 - 1 is 7.
8 - 2... Think, *2 and what make 8?* (6) 8 - 2 is 6.
8 - 3... Think, *3 and what make 8?* (5) 8 - 3 is 5.

(Chorus)

8 - 4... Think, *4 and what make 8?* (4) 8 - 4 is 4.
8 - 5... Think, *5 and what make 8?* (3) 8 - 5 is 3.
8 - 6... Think, *6 and what make 8?* (2) 8 - 6 is 2.

(Chorus)

8 - 7... Think, *7 and what make 8?* (1) 8 - 7 is 1.
8 - 8... You don't need to think about this one.
Any number minus itself is what?
Any number minus itself is always zero.

(Chorus)

Let us practice this concept with our facts of 9.
Let us think *addition* as the answer we'll find.
I will say the problem. Just follow my lead.
It's the only way to learn, don't you agree?

9 - 1... Think, *1 and what make 9?* (8) 9 - 1 is 8.
9 - 2... Think, *2 and what make 9?* (7) 9 - 2 is 7.
9 - 3... Think, *3 and what make 9?* (6) 9 - 3 is 6.

(Chorus)

9 - 4... Think, *4 and what make 9?* (5) 9 - 4 is 5.
9 - 5... Think, *5 and what make 9?* (4) 9 - 5 is 4.
9 - 6... Think, *6 and what make 9?* (3) 9 - 6 is 3.

(Chorus)

9 - 7... Think, *7 and what make 9?* (2) 9 - 7 is 2.
9 - 8... Think, *8 and what make 9?* (1) 9 - 8 is 1.
Any number minus itself is what?
Any number minus itself is always zero.

(Chorus)

When you are solving a problem
and you need to subtract,
I want you to think *addition facts*.

Oh yeah, think addition facts.
Think addition facts. Just think addition facts.

Minuends 8, 9

8	8	8	8	8	8	8	8	8	9
- 0	- 1	- 2	- 3	- 4	- 5	- 6	- 7	- 8	- 0

9	9	9	9	9	9	9	9	9	9
- 1	- 2	- 3	- 4	- 5	- 6	- 7	- 8	- 9	- 2

8	8	9	8	9	8	9	8	9	8
- 5	- 2	- 1	- 3	- 6	- 8	- 4	- 7	- 8	- 0

9	9	8	9	8	9	8	9	8	9
- 1	- 7	- 6	- 2	- 5	- 0	- 4	- 3	- 8	- 9

8	8	9	8	9	8	9	8	9	9
- 3	- 6	- 2	- 3	- 4	- 5	- 1	- 7	- 5	- 8

9	9	8	9	8	9	8	9	8	8
- 1	- 7	- 4	- 6	- 2	- 2	- 6	- 8	- 7	- 3

Subtraction ▭ Search

Write the difference. Find and circle each complete subtraction sentence in the puzzle below. Search horizontally or vertically.

8-0=	8-5=	7-1=	7-6=	6-3=	5-1=	4-0=	3-0=	2-1=
8-1=	8-6=	7-2=5	7-7=	6-4=	5-2=	4-1=	3-1=	2-2=
8-2=	8-7=	7-3=	6-0=	6-5=	5-3=	4-2=	3-2=	1-0=
8-3=	8-8=	7-4=	6-1=	6-6=	5-4=	4-3=	3-3=	1-1=
8-4=	7-0=	7-5=	6-2=	5-0=	5-5=	4-4=	2-0=	

1	8	-	0	=	8	5	1	3	5	8	-	7	=	1
2	-	5	8	2	-	9	7	6	6	-	5	-	0	9
4	8	8	5	-	1	=	4	7	-	4	=	3	6	1
-	=	2	-	9	=	8	1	0	4	=	2	=	9	-
0	0	1	0	8	7	5	2	5	=	4	8	4	9	0
=	5	6	=	8	1	0	-	8	2	0	2	7	6	=
4	3	8	5	-	5	=	0	1	4	9	6	5	2	1
9	4	2	1	6	0	2	=	9	-	6	-	6	=	0
7	6	4	2	-	9	0	2	-	1	=	1	-	9	8
7	-	7	=	0	6	5	2	3	=	8	-	2	=	6
8	8	9	0	=	1	3	4	9	3	8	4	=	3	3
2	3	8	5	6	6	7	-	0	=	7	6	4	9	9
-	7	-	8	9	7	-	9	0	5	6	4	-	8	2
2	1	5	7	6	-	5	=	1	8	9	0	4	2	3
=	9	=	8	5	5	=	2	4	7	-	2	=	5	8
0	7	3	6	5	-	2	=	3	0	3	-	0	=	3
0	4	9	7	6	5	2	0	8	5	2	7	0	0	-
6	-	8	5	3	1	8	1	4	-	2	=	2	9	1
5	3	-	3	=	0	-	6	5	3	0	1	9	6	=
8	=	6	4	7	-	6	=	1	=	8	4	6	5	2
-	1	9	0	6	5	=	6	-	2	9	7	-	1	0
3	7	8	1	3	-	2	=	1	7	7	-	1	=	6
=	3	5	-	4	=	1	8	=	6	4	3	=	5	9
5	6	-	3	=	3	9	0	0	7	9	0	5	8	7

We are learning our facts, our facts of 10.
We are "thinking addition" all over again.
I'll say a number. Think, *How many more
will get you to ten?* Now it's time to explore.

Chorus
The facts of ten. The facts of ten.
Think, *How many more will get you to ten?*
The facts of ten. The facts of ten.
We'll say them again and again.

6...how many more will get you to ten? (4)
8...how many more will get you to ten? (2)
5...how many more will get you to ten? (5)
3...how many more will get you to ten? (7)
9...how many more will get you to ten? (1)
2...how many more will get you to ten? (8)
4...how many more will get you to ten? (6)
7...how many more will get you to ten? (3)

(Chorus)

10 - 1 is 9, so 1 + 9 is 10
10 - 2 is 8, so 2 + 8 is 10
10 - 3 is 7, so 3 + 7 is 10
10 - 4 is 6, so 4 + 6 is 10
10 - 5 is 5, so 5 + 5 is 10
10 - 6 is 4, so 6 + 4 is 10
10 - 7 is 3, so 7 + 3 is 10
10 - 8 is 2, so 8 + 2 is 10
10 - 9 is 1, so 9 + 1 is 10 and 10 - 10 is 0

(Chorus)

10 - 10 is 0   10 - 9 is 1
10 - 8 is 2   10 - 7 is 3
10 - 6 is 4   10 - 5 is 5
10 - 4 is 6   10 - 3 is 7
10 - 2 is 8   10 - 1 is 9

(Chorus)

Minuend 10

10	10	10	10	10	10	10	10	10	10
- 0	- 1	- 2	- 3	- 4	- 5	- 6	- 7	- 8	- 9

10	10	10	10	10	10	10	10	10	10
- 10	- 9	- 2	- 3	- 4	- 10	- 6	- 2	- 8	- 10

10	10	10	10	10	10	10	10	10	10
- 5	- 2	- 1	- 5	- 4	- 3	- 6	- 8	- 4	- 7

10	10	10	10	10	10	10	10	10	10
- 8	- 0	- 9	- 7	- 6	- 2	- 6	- 5	- 0	- 4

10	10	10	10	10	10	10	10	10	10
- 3	- 6	- 2	- 3	- 9	- 5	- 1	- 7	- 5	- 8

10	10	10	10	10	10	10	10	10	10
- 1	- 7	- 4	- 6	- 2	- 8	- 6	- 9	- 7	- 3

Bowling by Subtraction

Write the difference.

10	10	10	10	10	10	10	10	10	10	10
- 0	- 1	- 2	- 3	- 4	- 5	- 6	- 7	- 8	- 9	- 10

Pretend you're bowling. Complete the subtraction sentence for each roll.
Each red pin will be knocked down. How many will be left standing?

   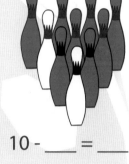

10 - ___ = ___   10 - ___ = ___   10 - ___ = ___   10 - ___ = ___

 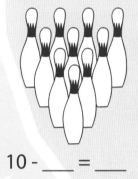  

10 - ___ = ___   10 - ___ = ___   10 - ___ = ___   10 - ___ = ___

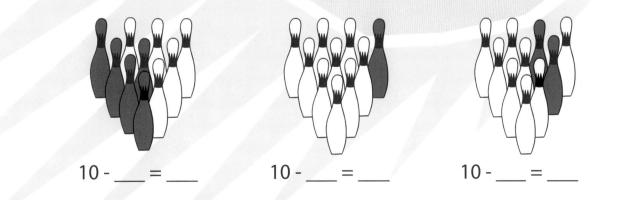

10 - ___ = ___   10 - ___ = ___   10 - ___ = ___

25

Cross-Number Puzzler

Write each complete subtraction
sentence in the "cross-number" puzzle.

Across

5. 4 - 2 = ___
7. 10 - 6 = ___
9. 10 - 8 = ___
11. 8 - 7 = ___
12. 4 - 4 = ___
15. 5 - 4 = ___
16. 8 - 4 = ___
19. 6 - 3 = ___
20. 8 - 8 = ___
23. 9 - 2 = ___
24. 6 - 6 = ___
26. 7 - 1 = ___
27. 6 - 5 = ___
32. 6 - 4 = ___
33. 10 - 5 = ___
34. 2 - 1 = ___
35. 10 - 7 = ___
36. 3 - 3 = ___
37. 9 - 6 = ___
39. 10 - 4 = ___
40. 5 - 4 = ___
42. 4 - 3 = ___
45. 7 - 3 = ___
47. 10 - 9 = ___
48. 7 - 5 = ___

Down

1. 8 - 5 = ___
2. 10 - 10 = ___
3. 7 - 7 = ___
4. 9 - 5 = ___
6. 4 - 1 = ___
8. 6 - 2 = ___
10. 9 - 7 = ___
11. 8 - 3 = ___
13. 2 - 2 = ___
14. 3 - 1 = ___
17. 5 - 3 = ___
18. 7 - 4 = ___
21. 6 - 1 = ___
22. 7 - 2 = ___
25. 8 - 6 = ___
26. 7 - 6 = ___
28. 10 - 1 = ___
29. 3 - 2 = ___
30. 9 - 6 = ___
31. 5 - 2 = ___
33. 10 - 3 = ___
37. 9 - 9 = ___
38. 5 - 5 = ___
39. 10 - 2 = ___
41. 8 - 2 = ___
43. 9 - 8 = ___
44. 9 - 1 = ___
46. 8 - 1 = ___

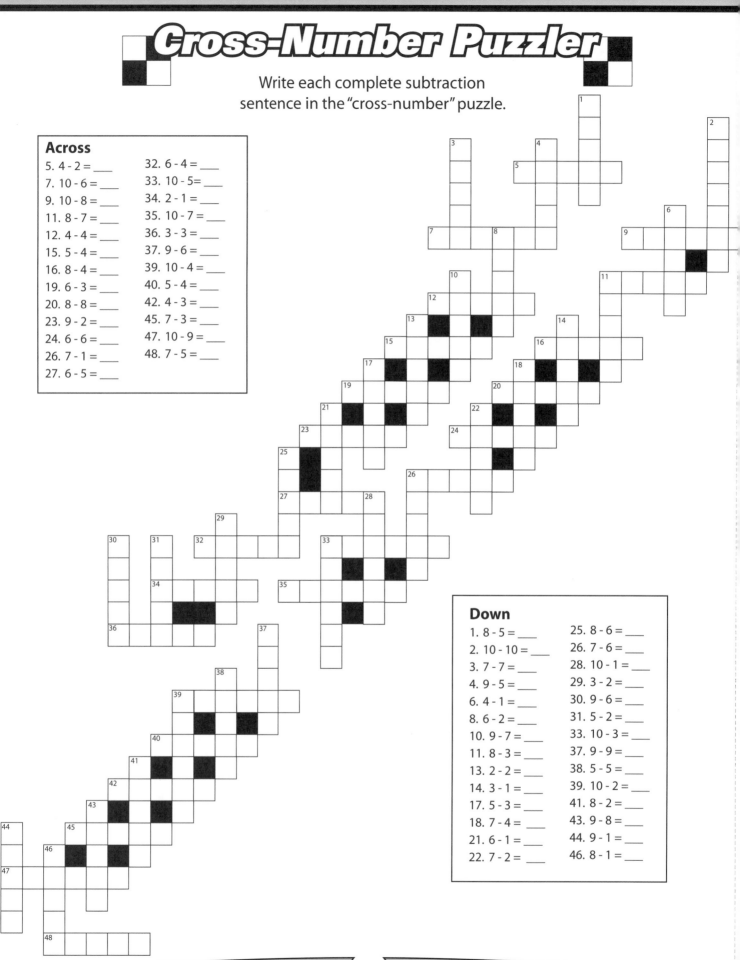

26

Just Add +1 More!

#8

The "get to ten" strategy that you learned in the last song will help you learn the facts of 11. Look at the problem 11 - 7. Think in your head, *7 plus what will get me to 10?* Then, add one more. 7 + 3 =10 and 3 + 1 is 4. So 11 - 7 is 4. Look at 11 - 5. 5 plus what equals 10? Yes, 5 + 5 =10. Now add one more. Great. 5 + 1 = 6. So 11 - 5 = 6. If you practice the "get to 10" strategy and add one more, it will help you learn the facts of 11.

Chorus
Get up to ten and add one more.
Get up to ten and add one more.
If you think in your head, *Just get to ten,*
you can add one more, and then
the facts of eleven you'll memorize.
For it's smart and wise to strategize.
For learning math facts, I must confide,
will make you feel so good inside!

11 - 8...think, *8 plus what equals 10? 2!*
And 2 + 1 = 3, so 11 - 8 = 3.

11 - 4...think, *4 plus what equals 10? 6!*
And 6 + 1 = 7, so 11 - 4 = 7.

(Chorus)

The facts of eleven–are you ready to try?
Let's say each one. For you can rely
on what you've learned. Be confident–
for you are really intelligent!

11 - 1 is 10	11 - 2 is 9	11 - 3 is 8
11 - 4 is 7	11 - 5 is 6	11 - 6 is 5
11 - 7 is 4	11 - 8 is 3	11 - 9 is 2

One more time.

11 - 1 is 10	11 - 4 is 7	11 - 7 is 4
11 - 2 is 9	11 - 5 is 6	11 - 8 is 3
11 - 3 is 8	11 - 6 is 5	11 - 9 is 2

(Chorus)

Get up to ten and add one more.
Get up to ten and add one more.
Get up to ten and add one more.
It's a strategy you can't ignore!

Minuend 11

11	11	11	11	11	11	11	11	11	11
- 0	- 1	- 2	- 3	- 4	- 5	- 6	- 7	- 8	- 9

11	11	11	11	11	11	11	11	11	11
- 10	- 11	- 3	- 4	- 9	- 6	- 2	- 8	- 11	- 5

11	11	11	11	11	11	11	11	11	11
- 5	- 2	- 1	- 3	- 6	- 10	- 4	- 7	- 8	- 11

11	11	11	11	11	11	11	11	11	11
- 9	- 7	- 6	- 2	- 5	- 0	- 4	- 3	- 8	- 11

11	11	11	11	11	11	11	11	11	11
- 3	- 10	- 2	- 3	- 9	- 11	- 1	- 7	- 5	- 8

11	11	11	11	11	11	11	11	11	11
- 1	- 7	- 11	- 6	- 2	- 8	- 6	- 9	- 7	- 3

28

NUMBER LINE
SUBTRACTION

Finish drawing each subtraction sentence on the number line. Write the missing subtrahend.

0	1	2	3	4	5	6	7	8	9	10	11	12	13

11 - _7_ **= 4**

0	1	2	3	4	5	6	7	8	9	10	11	12	13

8 - ____ **= 3**

0	1	2	3	4	5	6	7	8	9	10	11	12	13

10 - ____ **= 8**

0	1	2	3	4	5	6	7	8	9	10	11	12	13

9 - ____ **= 5**

0	1	2	3	4	5	6	7	8	9	10	11	12	13

11 - ____ **= 8**

0	1	2	3	4	5	6	7	8	9	10	11	12	13

8 - ____ **= 4**

0	1	2	3	4	5	6	7	8	9	10	11	12	13

9 - ____ **= 7**

0	1	2	3	4	5	6	7	8	9	10	11	12	13

10 - ____ **= 3**

0	1	2	3	4	5	6	7	8	9	10	11	12	13

11 - ____ **= 2**

#9

S-U-B-T-R-A-C-T-I-O-N

S-U-B-T-R-A-C-T-I-O-N. Subtraction. Yeah!
S-U-B-T-R-A-C-T-I-O-N. Subtraction. A-huh!
Subtraction facts we are going to shout
'cause math is something worth shouting about.
We'll say them fast, and we'll say them slow.
And when we're through, the facts we'll know.

Chorus
Subtraction facts. Subtraction facts.
Take away and minus–we're talkin' cool math.
Subtraction facts. Subtraction facts.
Are you ready to learn subtraction facts?

12 - 1 is 11	12 - 4 is 8	12 - 7 is 5
12 - 2 is 10	12 - 5 is 7	12 - 8 is 4
12 - 3 is 9	12 - 6 is 6	12 - 9 is 3

S-U-B-T-R-A-C-T-I-O-N. Subtraction. Yeah!
S-U-B-T-R-A-C-T-I-O-N. Subtraction. A-huh!
Now say the facts of 12 again.
A little faster we'll go, and then
we'll learn our facts–each and every one.
And while we're at it, we'll have some fun!

12 - 1 is 11	12 - 2 is 10	12 - 3 is 9
12 - 4 is 8	12 - 5 is 7	12 - 6 is 6
12 - 7 is 5	12 - 8 is 4	12 - 9 is 3

(Chorus)

13 - 1 is 12	13 - 2 is 11	13 - 3 is 10
13 - 4 is 9	13 - 5 is 8	13 - 6 is 7
13 - 7 is 6	13 - 8 is 5	13 - 9 is 4

S-U-B-T-R-A-C-T-I-O-N. Subtraction. Yeah!
S-U-B-T-R-A-C-T-I-O-N. Subtraction. A-huh!
Now say the facts of 13 again.
A little faster we'll go, and then
we'll learn our facts–each and every one.
And while we're at it, we'll have some fun!

13 - 1 is 12	13 - 2 is 11	13 - 3 is 10
13 - 4 is 9	13 - 5 is 8	13 - 6 is 7
13 - 7 is 6	13 - 8 is 5	13 - 9 is 4

(Chorus)

TIP: Try the "Subtracting Five" trick. When you are subtracting five from a two-digit basic fact, you just add the numerals in the one's place. For example, in the problem 13 - 5, you add the numbers in the one's place: 5 + 3 = 8. 8 is the answer.

30

Minuend 12, 13

12	12	12	12	12	12	12	12	12	12
- 0	- 1	- 2	- 3	- 4	- 5	- 6	- 7	- 8	- 9

12	12	12	13	13	13	13	13	13	13
- 10	- 11	- 12	- 0	- 1	- 2	- 3	- 4	- 5	- 6

13	13	13	13	13	13	13	12	12	13
- 7	- 8	- 9	- 10	- 11	- 12	- 13	- 7	- 9	- 0

12	13	12	13	13	12	12	13	12	13
- 9	- 7	- 6	- 2	- 5	- 0	- 4	- 3	- 8	- 12

12	12	13	12	12	13	12	13	12	13
- 3	- 10	- 8	- 3	- 9	- 12	- 1	- 7	- 5	- 4

12	13	12	12	13	12	12	12	12	13
- 1	- 6	- 12	- 6	- 9	- 2	- 11	- 9	- 10	- 3

Fact Families

Fact families. Fact families. (Repeat)

We're part of a family–the math facts crew.
We all work together to really help you.

To figure out problems, we all do relate.
We all work together. We're friendly classmates.

Chorus
Fact families. Fact families.
Look at three numbers and you will agree.

Take 14 and 6 and then number 8.
I'll show you how these numbers relate.

Let's take the numbers 14, 6, and 8.
Do you know that you can make two addition
problems and two subtraction problems
with these numbers? You can.
14 – 6 is 8 and 14 – 8 is 6.
6 + 8 is 14 and 8 + 6 is 14.
These numbers are a "fact family."

(Chorus)

Take 14 and 4 and then number 10.
I'll show you a special fact family again.

14 – 4 is 10 and 14 – 10 is 4.
4 + 10 is 14 and 10 + 4 is 14.
Let's practice our facts of fourteen, and
then you can practice making fact families.

14 – 1 is 13   14 – 2 is 12   14 – 3 is 11
14 – 4 is 10   14 – 5 is 9   14 – 6 is 8
14 – 7 is 7   14 – 8 is 6   14 – 9 is 5

Let's say them again.

14 – 1 is 13   14 – 2 is 12   14 – 3 is 11
14 – 4 is 10   14 – 5 is 9   14 – 6 is 8
14 – 7 is 7   14 – 8 is 6   14 – 9 is 5

We're part of a family–the math facts crew.
We all work together to really help you.

To figure out problems, we all do relate.
We all work together. We're friendly classmates.

(Chorus)

That taking these numbers and making
some facts will help you learn addition
and subtraction math.

Fact families. Fact families. (Repeat)

TIP: Try out the cool "Nine Trick!" when subtracting 9 from a basic fact. When the top number is a two-digit number (10, 11, 12, 13, 14, 15, 16, 17, or 18), add the top two numbers horizontally. For example in the problem 16 - 9, you know that you are subtracting 9, but look at the top number, 16, and think: 6 + 1 = 7. So 7 is the answer.

Minuend 14

14	14	14	14	14	14	14	14	14	14
- 0	- 1	- 2	- 3	- 4	- 5	- 6	- 7	- 8	- 9

14	14	14	14	14	14	14	14	14	14
- 10	- 11	- 12	- 13	- 14	- 2	- 3	- 4	- 5	- 6

14	14	14	14	14	14	14	14	14	14
- 7	- 8	- 9	- 10	- 11	- 12	- 13	- 7	- 9	- 0

14	14	14	14	14	14	14	14	14	14
- 9	- 7	- 6	- 2	- 5	- 0	- 4	- 3	- 8	- 14

14	14	14	14	14	14	14	14	14	14
- 3	- 10	- 8	- 13	- 9	- 14	- 1	- 7	- 5	- 4

14	14	14	14	14	14	14	14	14	14
- 1	- 6	- 14	- 6	- 9	- 2	- 11	- 9	- 10	- 13

33

Fact Families

Fact families are 3 numbers that are "related" and make 2 addition sentences and 2 subtraction sentences. For example— 3,4,7:

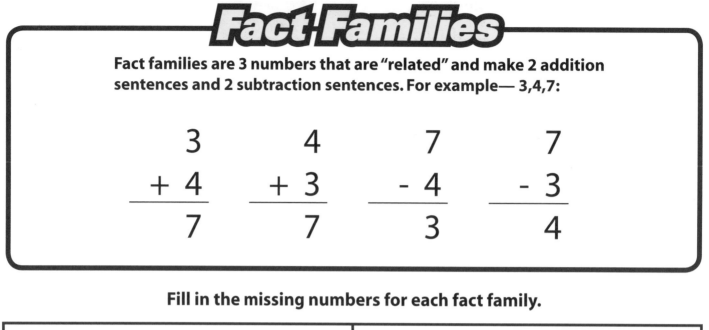

$$\begin{array}{r} 3 \\ + 4 \\ \hline 7 \end{array} \qquad \begin{array}{r} 4 \\ + 3 \\ \hline 7 \end{array} \qquad \begin{array}{r} 7 \\ - 4 \\ \hline 3 \end{array} \qquad \begin{array}{r} 7 \\ - 3 \\ \hline 4 \end{array}$$

Fill in the missing numbers for each fact family.

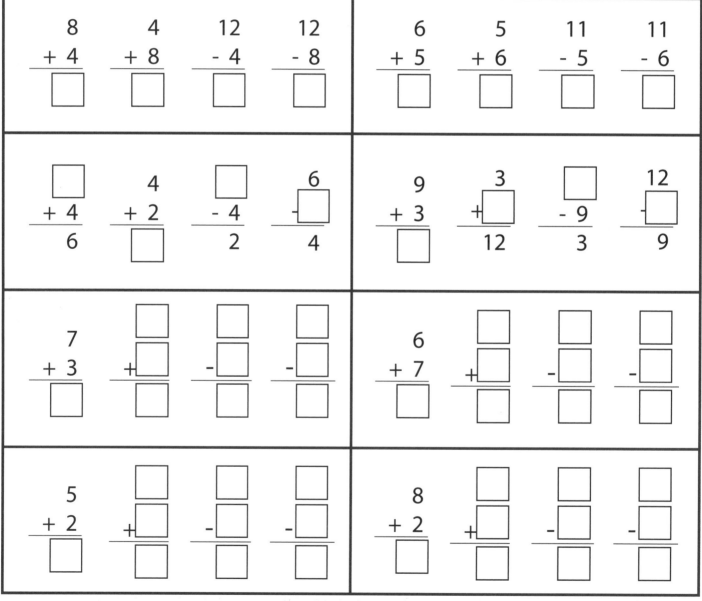

More Fact Families

Practice Fact Families! Roll the 20-sided dice.
Write the numbers in the first two squares. Now
find the third number of the fact family. Then
write the Fact Family using those three numbers.

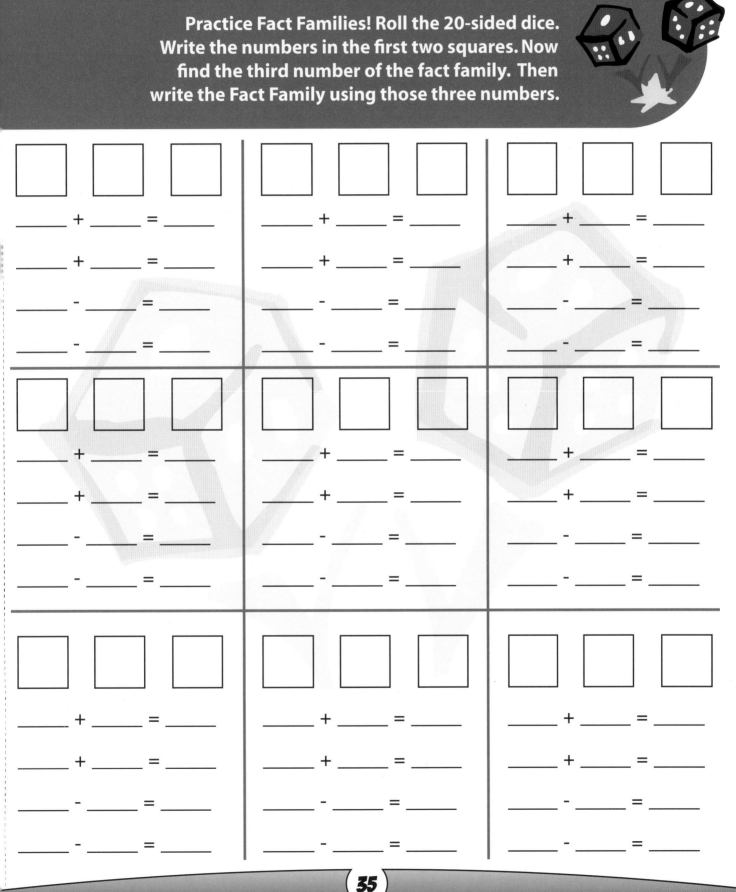

_____ + _____ = _____

_____ + _____ = _____

_____ - _____ = _____

_____ - _____ = _____

_____ + _____ = _____

_____ + _____ = _____

_____ - _____ = _____

_____ - _____ = _____

_____ + _____ = _____

_____ + _____ = _____

_____ - _____ = _____

_____ - _____ = _____

_____ + _____ = _____

_____ + _____ = _____

_____ - _____ = _____

_____ - _____ = _____

_____ + _____ = _____

_____ + _____ = _____

_____ - _____ = _____

_____ - _____ = _____

_____ + _____ = _____

_____ + _____ = _____

_____ - _____ = _____

_____ - _____ = _____

_____ + _____ = _____

_____ + _____ = _____

_____ - _____ = _____

_____ - _____ = _____

_____ + _____ = _____

_____ + _____ = _____

_____ - _____ = _____

_____ - _____ = _____

_____ + _____ = _____

_____ + _____ = _____

_____ - _____ = _____

_____ - _____ = _____

#11 Say It Again Say It Again

Chorus
Say it, say it, say it again.
Drill the facts. Repeat them all.
Get them in your head.
(Repeat)

Repetition is the key once you know the rules.
So, say each one after me. It's a great learning tool.

15 – 1 is 14   (15 – 1 is 14)   15 – 2 is 13   (15 – 2 is 13)
15 – 3 is 12   (15 – 3 is 12)   15 – 4 is 11   (15 – 4 is 11)
15 – 5 is 10   (15 – 5 is 10)   15 – 6 is 9 (15 – 6 is 9)
15 – 7 is 8 (15 – 7 is 8)   15 – 8 is 7 (15 – 8 is 7)
15 – 9 is 6 (15 – 9 is 6)

(Chorus)

Repetition is the key, so further up we go.
Say each one after me. Become a subtraction pro.

16 – 1 is 15   (16 – 1 is 15)   16 – 2 is 14   (16 – 2 is 14)
16 – 3 is 13   (16 – 3 is 13)   16 – 4 is 12   (16 – 4 is 12)
16 – 5 is 11   (16 – 5 is 11)   16 – 6 is 10   (16 – 6 is 10)
16 – 7 is 9 (16 – 7 is 9)   16 – 8 is 8 (16 – 8 is 8)
16 – 9 is 7 (16 – 9 is 7)

(Chorus)

Say it.

Say It Again Say It Aga
ay It Again Say It Aga

36

Minuends 15, 16

15	15	15	15	15	15	15	15	15	15
- 0	- 1	- 2	- 3	- 4	- 5	- 6	- 7	- 8	- 9

15	15	15	15	15	15	16	16	16	16
- 10	- 11	- 12	- 13	- 14	- 15	- 0	- 1	- 2	- 3

16	16	16	16	16	16	16	16	16	16
- 4	- 5	- 6	- 7	- 8	- 9	- 10	- 11	- 12	- 13

16	16	16	15	16	15	16	15	16	15
- 14	- 15	- 16	- 2	- 5	- 0	- 4	- 3	- 8	- 14

15	15	15	16	15	15	16	15	16	15
- 3	- 10	- 8	- 13	- 9	- 14	- 1	- 7	- 5	- 4

16	16	16	15	16	16	15	16	15	16
- 1	- 6	- 14	- 6	- 9	- 2	- 11	- 9	- 10	- 13

37

Secret Code

To find the answer, subtract the numbers, write the difference, and write the letter or punctuation mark above the correct difference below.

WHAT DID THE MATH BOOK SAY TO THE OTHER MATH BOOK?

! 15 – 0 = ___   **,** 16 – 5 = ___   **B** 15 – 7 = ___

E 15 – 15 = ___   **G** 16 – 14 = ___   **R** 15 – 12 = ___

I 15 – 9 = ___   **T** 16 – 12 = ___   **M** 16 – 3 = ___

S 16 – 15 = ___   **V** 15 – 8 = ___   **E** 16 – 6 = ___

L 16 – 7 = ___   **O** 15 – 10 = ___   **P** 16 – 4 = ___

O 16 – 11 = ___

___ ___ ___ ___   ___ ___ ___
6   11   7   0   2   5   4

___ ___ ___ ___ ___ ___ ___ ___ ___
12   3   5   8   9   0   13   1   15

Answer

Chorus
I can do it. (Yes, you can.)
I can do it. (Yes, you can.)
I can do it. (Yes, you can.)
Let's say them again and again and again.

Let's repeat each one in groups of three.
This memorizing thing can be easy.
If we say them again, it's called a repeat.
We'll learn the facts of seventeen.

17 – 1 is 16   17 – 2 is 15   17 – 3 is 14

Now repeat each one again and again.
17 – 1 is 16   17 – 2 is 15   17 – 3 is 14

(Chorus)

17 – 4 is 13   17 – 5 is 12   17 – 6 is 11

Now repeat each one again and again.
17 – 4 is 13   17 – 5 is 12   17 – 6 is 11

(Chorus)

Let's repeat each one in groups of three.
This memorizing thing can be easy.
If we say them again, it's called a repeat.
We'll learn the facts of seventeen.

17 – 7 is 10   17 – 8 is 9   17 – 9 is 8

Now repeat each one again and again.
17 – 7 is 10   17 – 8 is 9   17 – 9 is 8

(Chorus)

Let's say them again and again and again.

Minuend 17

17	17	17	17	17	17	17	17	17	17
− 0	− 1	− 2	− 3	− 4	− 5	− 6	− 7	− 8	− 9

17	17	17	17	17	17	17	17	17	17
− 10	− 11	− 12	− 13	− 14	− 15	− 16	− 17	− 2	− 3

17	17	17	17	17	17	17	17	17	17
− 4	− 5	− 6	− 7	− 8	− 9	− 10	− 11	− 12	− 13

17	17	17	17	17	17	17	17	17	17
− 14	− 15	− 16	− 17	− 14	− 2	− 5	− 0	− 4	− 8

17	17	17	17	17	17	17	17	17	17
− 3	− 10	− 8	− 13	− 4	− 9	− 15	− 1	− 7	− 5

17	17	17	17	17	17	17	17	17	17
− 1	− 6	− 15	− 6	− 9	− 2	− 11	− 9	− 10	− 13

Follow My Lead

Chorus
Follow my lead. Follow my lead,
as we learn the hard facts of eighteen.
Follow my lead. Follow my lead.
It's time to listen and repeat.

18 – 1 is 17   (18 – 1 is 17)
18 – 2 is 16   (18 – 2 is 16)
18 – 3 is 15   (18 – 3 is 15)

(Chorus)

18 – 4 is 14   (18 – 4 is 14)
18 – 5 is 13   (18 – 5 is 13)
18 – 6 is 12   (18 – 6 is 12)

(Chorus)

18 – 7 is 11   (18 – 7 is 11)
18 – 8 is 10   (18 – 8 is 10)
18 – 9 is 9   (18 – 9 is 9)

(Chorus)

Say them with me. Say them with me,
as we learn the hard facts of eighteen.
Say them with me. Say them with me.
It's time to listen and repeat.

18 – 1 is 17   18 – 2 is 16   18 – 3 is 15
18 – 4 is 14   18 – 5 is 13   18 – 6 is 12
18 – 7 is 11   18 – 8 is 10   18 – 9 is 9

(Chorus 2x)

Minuend 18

18	18	18	18	18	18	18	18	18	18
- 0	- 1	- 2	- 3	- 4	- 5	- 6	- 7	- 8	- 9

18	18	18	18	18	18	18	18	18	18
- 10	- 11	- 12	- 13	- 14	- 15	- 16	- 17	- 18	- 3

18	18	18	18	18	18	18	18	18	18
- 4	- 5	- 6	- 7	- 8	- 9	- 10	- 11	- 12	- 13

18	18	18	18	18	18	18	18	18	18
- 14	- 15	- 16	- 17	- 14	- 2	- 5	- 0	- 4	- 8

18	18	18	18	18	18	18	18	18	18
- 3	- 10	- 8	- 13	- 4	- 9	- 15	- 1	- 7	- 5

18	18	18	18	18	18	18	18	18	18
- 1	- 6	- 15	- 6	- 9	- 2	- 11	- 9	- 10	- 13

42

Find and circle the subtraction sentences with the minuend 18. Place a – or = sign between the numbers to complete the subtraction sentence. The numbers and differences may be horizontal or vertical.

18 Sentence Search

18	18	18	18	18	18	18	18	18	18
- 0	- 1	- 2	- 3	- 4	- 5	- 6	- 7	- 8	- 9

18	18	18	18	18	18	18	18	18
- 10	- 11	- 12	- 13	- 14	- 15	- 16	- 17	- 18

18 – 9 = 9			18	14	4	17	18	6	12
13	18	12	6	11	12	18	16	2	2
3	18	0	18	5	18	2	18	13	5
18	3	18	10	8	15	16	18	16	2
7	10	18	18	0	7	18	7	6	0
11	12	10	1	9	14	18	3	15	12
3	7	18	17	1	18	5	13	14	10
12	18	11	7	3	7	18	15	3	8
18	4	14	1	16	18	8	10	4	0

SEQUENCES

The object of the game is to have **two sequences of four markers in a row**—up, down, or diagonally. To play, you'll need the 20-sided die and different markers—buttons, candies, pennies or other game pieces—for each player. **On your turn, roll the dice and subtract the smaller number from the larger number.** Say the problem out loud and place a marker on the correct difference. You'll need to watch the board carefully to stop another player from making a sequence.

1	9	17	1	8	14	2	6	18	11
11	2	8	16	2	9	15	3	7	10
4	12	18	7	15	3	10	16	4	8
14	5	13	4	6	14	4	11	17	5
7	15	6	14	18	5	13	5	12	1
16	8	16	7	15	6	4	12	6	13
7	17	9	17	8	16	7	3	11	7
14	8	1	10	1	9	17	8	2	10
18	15	9	2	11	2	10	1	9	1
8	4	16	10	3	12	3	11	2	10
12	9	5	17	11	4	13	4	12	3
15	13	10	6	1	12	5	14	5	13
17	16	14	11	18	2	13	6	15	6

Suggestion: Photocopy this page before cutting out the cards.

SUBTRACTION BINGO

Practice your subtraction facts 0 - 18 with a partner. Each player selects a Bingo card. Make additional bingo cards for more fun. **Roll the two 20-sided dice. Subtract the numbers rolled**—the smaller number from the larger number. Players place a marker on the correct difference. The first player to have five in a row yells "BINGO!"

BINGO

B	I	N	G	O
4	13	10	17	6
9	18	5	3	7
8	2	0	8	16
7	5	12	15	6
14	11	4	3	1

BINGO

B	I	N	G	O
1	11	3	15	8
2	9	8	4	17
5	16	0	9	12
13	10	17	6	3
18	7	1	14	10

BINGO

B	I	N	G	O
9	1	18	14	4
15	7	2	10	9
6	3	0	12	16
12	11	5	1	8
7	17	3	13	5

BINGO

B	I	N	G	O
2	8	10	4	12
4	15	11	6	1
7	18	0	8	13
14	3	6	9	16
10	5	2	17	1

This page was intentionally left blank for the "Subtraction Bingo" Game to be completed.

Subtraction Table Race 1-10

Time yourself to see how quickly you can complete the **Subtrction Table**! Before completing the chart, you may want to **photocopy** the page so that you can practice many times! For more fun, play this game with one or more friends. The first player fills in any square on the **Subtraction Table**. The next player fills in another square. It is important to watch carefully what the other players write; if a player makes a mistake, another player may correct it on his or her turn. How quickly can you fill in all the squares!

−	1	2	3	4	5	6	7	8	9	10
1										
2										
3										
4										
5										
6										
7										
8										
9										
10										

Subtraction Table Race 10-18

Time yourself to see how quickly you can complete the **Subtraction Table**! Before completing the chart, you may want to **photocopy** the page so that you can practice many times! For more fun, play this game with one or more friends. The first player fills in any square on the **Subtraction Table**. The next player fills in another square. It is important to watch carefully what the other players write; if a player makes a mistake, another player may correct it on his or her turn. How quickly can you fill in all the squares!

−	10	11	12	13	14	15	16	17	18
10									
11									
12									
13									
14									
15									
16									
17									
18									

TRIANGLES

Cut out and match the subtraction facts to the answers. Glue the pieces
on poster board or cardboard. Store the pieces in a plastic sandwich bag.

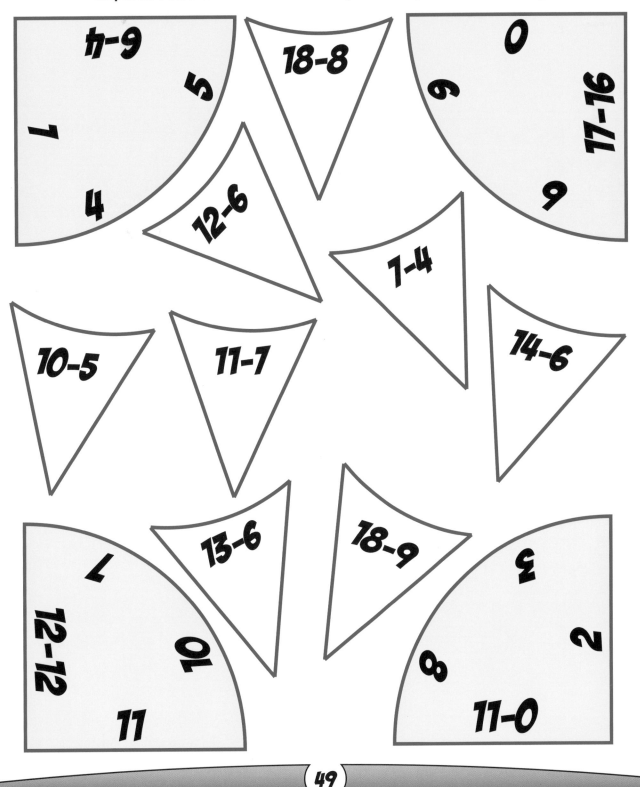

This page was intentionally left blank for the "Triangles" Game to be completed.

Calculator Race

The object of the game is to beat the calculator! You'll need three players. One player says subtraction sentence from the game board below. The second player finds the difference with the calculator. The third player finds the difference without a calculator. Player one decides who solved the problem first and places that player's initials in the box. Before playing, you may want to photocopy this page so you can play again and again

17 - 9	14 - 6	9 - 2	10 - 3	5 - 4	8 - 5	15 - 6	11 - 7	8 - 8	16 - 9
13 - 12	11 - 9	9 - 2	7 - 3	4 - 4	12 - 5	18 - 6	10 - 7	5 - 2	3 - 0
18 - 14	12 - 11	11 - 6	8 - 4	10 - 8	15 - 9	9 - 4	7 - 1	12 - 8	7 - 6
10 - 0	18 - 12	13 - 9	12 - 3	6 - 4	9 - 5	14 - 8	3 - 3	16 - 8	13 - 9
7 - 7	12 - 3	14 - 3	18 - 5	8 - 2	10 - 5	11 - 6	14 - 7	4 - 4	12 - 0
16 - 7	13 - 12	10 - 2	7 - 3	5 - 4	9 - 5	14 - 6	11 - 7	6 - 2	5 - 1
12 - 8	16 - 17	18 - 5	15 - 3	10 - 6	11 - 5	15 - 6	9 - 7	6 - 6	16 - 9
17 - 14	7 - 1	9 - 2	10 - 3	18 - 4	12 - 5	11 - 6	8 - 7	9 - 8	16 - 9
14 - 12	8 - 7	10 - 2	15 - 3	11 - 4	18 - 5	9 - 6	12 - 7	8 - 8	8 - 2
16 - 14	18 - 6	9 - 2	12 - 9	9 - 4	8 - 5	11 - 6	7 - 7	9 - 8	18 - 9

SUBTRACTION LEARNING GAMES

Subtraction WAR!

This twist on the classic card game, War, makes practicing subtraction facts even more fun! The game is played in much the way the traditional card game is played. However, players subtract the smaller number from the larger number they reveal. Each number card is worth its face value. The Ace has a value of 1. You may want to remove the face cards. However, if you leave them in the deck, decide what values those cards might have. For example all face cards might have a value of 12; a jack might have a value of 11, a queen might have a value of 12, and a king might have a value of 15. Shuffle the deck of cards and place it face down. Players draw a card from the top of the deck and reveal them at the same time. When both cards are revealed, the first player to subtract the smaller number from the larger number wins those two cards. For example, if players reveal a 5 of diamonds and a 9 of hearts, the first player to call out "4" wins those two cards. Play until one player has all the cards! **Option: Players each turn over two cards and subtract the smaller number from the larger number. The player with the lowest difference wins all four cards!**

Subtraction By The Bell

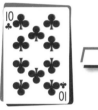

Challenge your classmates and practice your subtraction facts together with this noisy game! Ahead of time, write 25, 50 or more subtraction problems on index cards—one problem on each card. Place the homemade flashcards face down on the table. You'll need a bell, buzzer, or some other noisemaker. To play, divide your friends into two teams. The first players from each team stand with their hands ready to ring the bell. You turn over the top subtraction problem card. As soon as a player knows the answer he or she rings the bell. The first student to ring the bell gets to say the answer; if correct he or she earns a point for the team. If a player hesitates or calls out the wrong answer, the other team receives the point. Play continues with the next two players. The first team to earn 25 or 50 points is the winner.

Subtraction TANGLER

You and your friends will have fun practicing your subtraction facts with this version of the classic party game. First, make a set of large Difference cards (0 – 18) out of construction paper or poster board. Next, make a smaller deck of subtraction problems, leaving off the difference. Place the Difference cards face up on the floor. The announcer reads the top Problem card and adds an instruction. For example, "9 – 3 = ___, Place your right hand on the difference." The first player places his or her right hand on the number 6. The announcer reads the next Problem card and adds an instruction. For example, 7 – 4 = ___. Place your left foot on the difference. The second player places his or her left foot on the number 3. Players must keep this position until the announcer gives a new instruction. Play until everyone falls in a heap!

SKUNK

You and a small group of friends will quickly pass the time—and practice your subtraction—with this classic game of strategy and chance. To play, you'll need the 20-sided dice from page 95, pencils, and paper. Take turns rolling the dice and subtracting the smaller number from the larger number. Your points are equal to the difference. You can roll as many times as you want, but if you roll a difference equal to 1, you lose all your points for that turn. When you choose to stop, write your score and pass the die to the next player. The first player to reach 100 points wins.

DOMINO Subtraction

You'll need a set of dominoes for this great practice. Draw a domino and subtract the smaller number from the larger number. For more challenging play, draw two dominoes; look at each as a two-digit number. Subtract the smaller two-digit number from the larger two-digit number. If you want, play for points adding the difference each round.

Grab Bag

Choose a number to work with. Put that many objects into a bag—crayons, buttons, beans, candies. Players take turns pulling objects out of the bag. The other player must calculate how many objects are left inside the bag and write the number sentence. Then check inside the bag to learn if the player is correct.

Subtraction

Subtraction Tic Tac Toe

Draw a standard tic tac toe grid. Instead of using Xs and Os, players use the numbers 0 through 9 or 0 through 12. Each number can be used only once during a game. The object of the game is to complete any row, column or diagonal so that the difference of two of the three numbers equals the third number. The first move may NOT be in the center; the second and subsequent moves, however, can be anywhere on the grid.

More or Less

Practice your subtraction facts with this fast-paced card game! You'll need a standard deck of playing cards. King = 13, Queen = 12, and Jack = 11. Deal all the cards to the players. The first player says, "I have a ___; who has ____ less?" For example, if the player has an eight, he could say, "I have an eight; who has two less?" The first player with a card that corresponds correctly to the equation says, "I do!" The two players discard the cards in the subtraction sentence. The first player to discard all of his or her cards is the winner!

Subtraction Bowling

Practice subtraction facts with a simple game of bowling. Use one or more sets of inexpensive plastic bowling pins. Make your own pins from household items that can be easily knocked over—cans, tissue boxes, playing blocks, etc. Roll a small ball toward the pins. Players must count the number of pins knocked down and subtract that number from the total. A correct answer allows the player to roll again. An incorrect answer ends a turn.

Breaking Eggs

Practice subtraction facts to 15 with a simple egg carton and 15 counters. The counters must be two-sided with a different color on each side. One color will represent broken eggs and the other color will represent unbroken eggs. Paint pennies, flat rocks, toy coins, or use small poster-board tiles. To begin, place the "eggs" unbroken side up in the carton. Close the lid, drop or shake the carton. Open the carton and say aloud the subtraction problem. "I started with 15 eggs. Seven are broken. Now, I have 5 left. 15 – 7 = 5." Play with a friend, taking turns breaking the eggs and saying the subtraction fact.

Subtraction 10

You'll need two players and the 20-sided dice from page 95. Both players roll one die. The player who rolled the highest number wins the round and subtracts the smaller number from the larger number. Write the difference as your score for the round. The winner is the player with the most points at the end of ten rounds.

Ring Toss Subtraction

Set up an inexpensive ring toss set—or any other carnival-type challenge. Players roll the two 20-sided dice and subtract the difference. With the correct answer the player earns the difference. The player then tosses the ring to the post—a ringer doubles the points. The first player to reach 100 points is the winner.

Compare and write < (less than), > (greater than), or = (equal) in the circle.

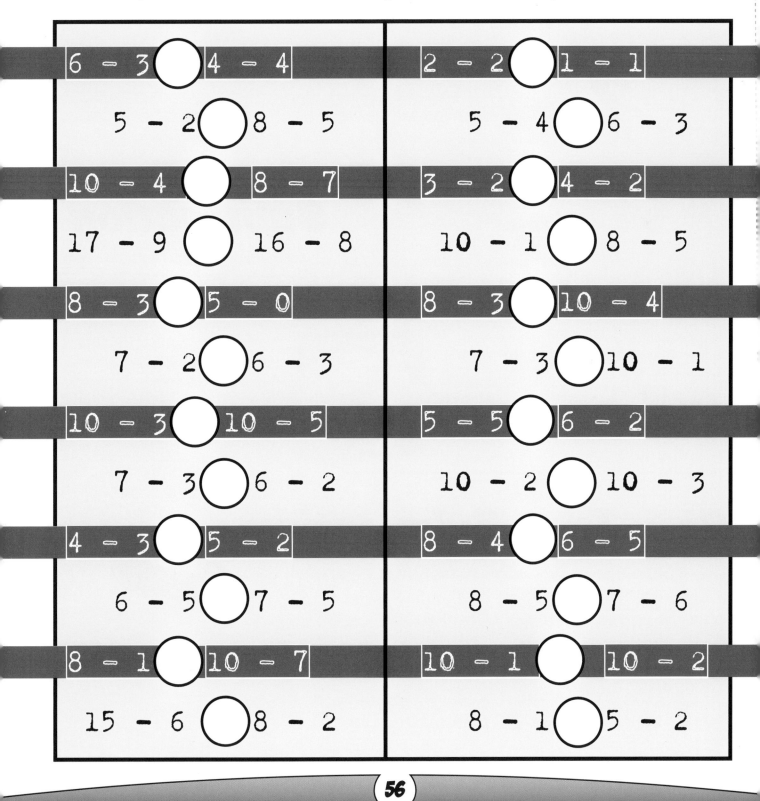

$6 - 3 \bigcirc 4 - 4$

$5 - 2 \bigcirc 8 - 5$

$10 - 4 \bigcirc 8 - 7$

$17 - 9 \bigcirc 16 - 8$

$8 - 3 \bigcirc 5 - 0$

$7 - 2 \bigcirc 6 - 3$

$10 - 3 \bigcirc 10 - 5$

$7 - 3 \bigcirc 6 - 2$

$4 - 3 \bigcirc 5 - 2$

$6 - 5 \bigcirc 7 - 5$

$8 - 1 \bigcirc 10 - 7$

$15 - 6 \bigcirc 8 - 2$

$2 - 2 \bigcirc 1 - 1$

$5 - 4 \bigcirc 6 - 3$

$3 - 2 \bigcirc 4 - 2$

$10 - 1 \bigcirc 8 - 5$

$8 - 3 \bigcirc 10 - 4$

$7 - 3 \bigcirc 10 - 1$

$5 - 5 \bigcirc 6 - 2$

$10 - 2 \bigcirc 10 - 3$

$8 - 4 \bigcirc 6 - 5$

$8 - 5 \bigcirc 7 - 6$

$10 - 1 \bigcirc 10 - 2$

$8 - 1 \bigcirc 5 - 2$

*MORE

< or > or =

Compare and write < (less than), > (greater than), or = (equal) in the circle.

17 − 10 ◯ 18 − 7		15 − 6 ◯ 10 − 1	
15 − 5 ◯ 15 − 4		18 − 15 ◯ 15 − 10	
16 − 15 ◯ 6 − 2		15 − 7 ◯ 16 − 5	
15 − 15 ◯ 16 − 6		15 − 6 ◯ 10 − 2	
15 − 5 ◯ 10 − 6		16 − 7 ◯ 17 − 10	
18 − 8 ◯ 15 − 2		10 − 3 ◯ 15 − 5	
17 − 12 ◯ 18 − 15		17 − 1 ◯ 18 − 0	
18 − 15 ◯ 17 − 4		18 − 4 ◯ 16 − 2	
16 − 10 ◯ 15 − 6		15 − 6 ◯ 17 − 8	
15 − 4 ◯ 17 − 8		15 − 3 ◯ 14 − 2	
17 − 5 ◯ 15 − 7		17 − 4 ◯ 15 − 1	
16 − 6 ◯ 18 − 7		16 − 3 ◯ 15 − 1	

Two-Digit Numbers Without Regrouping

1. Subtract the **ONES**.	2. Subtract the **TENS**.
36 - 12 ―― 4	36 - 12 ―― 24

Subtract the numbers and write the **difference**.

83 - 61	58 - 35	75 - 24	99 - 33	58 - 16
79 - 26	82 - 31	24 - 12	46 - 34	67 - 32
58 - 32	87 - 64	98 - 17	49 - 24	37 - 16
69 - 27	37 - 15	29 - 13	62 - 31	57 - 44

Two-Digit Numbers Without Regrouping

84 - 24	82 - 10	98 - 24	65 - 23	57 - 12
63 - 12	39 - 29	26 - 16	84 - 34	46 - 26
97 - 23	27 - 17	84 - 43	75 - 24	45 - 24
46 - 22	28 - 13	94 - 23	61 - 40	99 - 33
45 - 32	75 - 25	91 - 10	86 - 26	52 - 12

The Missing Number

Fill in the missing numbers.

45	75	89	52	67
-25	-3☐	-☐1	-1☐	-1☐
☐☐	44	48	41	☐2

9☐	☐6	24	62	99
-17	-3☐	-☐☐	-3☐	-☐3
81	12	12	☐1	6☐

54	4☐	6☐	75	☐5
-☐3	-24	-☐6	-1☐	-4☐
4☐	☐5	13	☐1	53

39	5☐	☐8	☐☐	63
-☐☐	-☐7	-2☐	-22	-☐3
11	41	55	66	3☐

9☐	28	☐5	5☐	67
-☐9	-☐☐	-2☐	-☐4	-23
80	14	10	22	☐☐

Two-Digit Numbers With Regrouping

1. Subtract the **ONES**. 3-4 cannot be done.	2. Take **1 ten** from the **tens**. **10+3=13** in the **ones**. **5** in the **tens**.	3. Now subtract. **13-4=9** in the **ones**. **5-2=3** in the **tens**.
63 - 24	5 13 6̸3 - 24	5 13 6̸3 - 24 39

TIP: More on top, no need to stop! More on the floor, go next door!
Subtract the numbers and write the **difference.**

83 - 64	54 - 28	33 - 18	68 - 49
71 - 53	42 - 27	63 - 17	31 - 18
94 - 56	82 - 63	53 - 24	67 - 28
41 - 19	62 - 38	75 - 27	84 - 17

Two-Digit Numbers With Regrouping

64 − 29	73 − 28	92 − 34	55 − 36	32 − 15
82 − 16	41 − 22	86 − 17	72 − 59	54 − 36
53 − 25	47 − 18	65 − 16	95 − 79	86 − 27
65 − 47	93 − 28	94 − 79	81 − 27	70 − 36
56 − 18	85 − 46	42 − 13	90 − 12	82 − 67

Three-Digit Numbers With Regrouping

1. Subtract the **ONES**. 6-7 cannot be done. Regroup 6 to 16 then subtract	2. Subtract the **tens**. 1 - 0 = 1	3. Subtract the **hundreds**. 3 - 2 = 1
$$\begin{array}{r} {}^{1}\ {}^{16} \\ 3\,2\,6 \\ -\,2\,0\,7 \\ \hline 9 \end{array}$$	$$\begin{array}{r} {}^{1}\ {}^{16} \\ 3\,2\,6 \\ -\,2\,0\,7 \\ \hline 1\,9 \end{array}$$	$$\begin{array}{r} {}^{1}\ {}^{16} \\ 3\,2\,6 \\ -\,2\,0\,7 \\ \hline 1\,1\,9 \end{array}$$

TIP: The BBB Rule-when the *BIG* number is on the *BOTTOM*, you *BORROW.*
Subtract the numbers and write the **difference.**

$$\begin{array}{r} 2\,9\,0 \\ -\,1\,8\,1 \\ \hline \end{array} \qquad \begin{array}{r} 8\,1\,7 \\ -\,1\,0\,9 \\ \hline \end{array} \qquad \begin{array}{r} 5\,6\,3 \\ -\,2\,4\,4 \\ \hline \end{array}$$

$$\begin{array}{r} 8\,5\,4 \\ -\,3\,2\,9 \\ \hline \end{array} \qquad \begin{array}{r} 5\,6\,3 \\ -\,4\,4\,7 \\ \hline \end{array} \qquad \begin{array}{r} 3\,6\,5 \\ -\,2\,5\,7 \\ \hline \end{array}$$

$$\begin{array}{r} 6\,4\,3 \\ -\,5\,2\,9 \\ \hline \end{array} \qquad \begin{array}{r} 4\,2\,8 \\ -\,3\,0\,9 \\ \hline \end{array} \qquad \begin{array}{r} 2\,2\,2 \\ -\,1\,0\,8 \\ \hline \end{array}$$

$$\begin{array}{r} 7\,5\,1 \\ -\,4\,4\,9 \\ \hline \end{array} \qquad \begin{array}{r} 5\,4\,8 \\ -\,1\,3\,9 \\ \hline \end{array} \qquad \begin{array}{r} 6\,3\,3 \\ -\,2\,1\,4 \\ \hline \end{array}$$

Three-Digit Numbers With Regrouping

592 -189	690 -617	497 -258	651 -242	882 -563
696 -238	952 -838	293 -144	740 -132	972 -549
482 -163	543 -235	781 -368	381 -257	250 -142
481 -347	981 -432	561 -136	670 -154	241 -128
773 -369	266 -117	497 -238	690 -281	781 -462

Calculator Race 2

Take the challenge to subtract two-digit and three-digit numbers! The object of the game is to beat the calculator! You'll need three players. One player says a subtraction sentence from the game board below. The second player solves the problem with the calculator. The third player solves the problem without a calculator. Player one decides who solved the problem first and places that player's initials in the box. Before playing, you may want to photocopy this page so you can play again and again.

135 - 127	94 - 56	39 - 22	73 - 18	659 - 457	428 - 317	845 - 245	313 - 174	187 - 122	85 - 24
248 - 129	792 - 582	684 - 441	788 - 321	444 - 257	643 - 386	972 - 648	159 - 127	371 - 158	866 - 857
67 - 14	873 - 119	99 - 34	743 - 387	109 - 87	55 - 22	63 - 18	783 - 549	198 - 127	68 - 39
150 - 129	881 - 538	138 - 119	263 - 100	82 - 47	98 - 58	144 - 112	53 - 21	872 - 728	63 - 29
350 - 237	75 - 24	631 - 229	183 - 57	86 - 49	763 - 578	111 - 65	87 - 76	982 - 835	120 - 69
455 - 337	166 - 85	83 - 27	789 - 393	552 - 546	997 - 874	59 - 31	187 - 68	677 - 559	52 - 43
46 - 38	608 - 370	173 - 59	255 - 138	109 - 62	148 - 59	856 - 628	906 - 719	665 - 68	167 - 99
717 - 348	562 - 222	889 - 721	231 - 139	882 - 557	123 - 56	101 - 68	558 - 372	92 - 18	68 - 19
443 - 245	870 - 771	184 - 96	570 - 99	111 - 44	286 - 159	973 - 688	339 - 171	84 - 28	881 - 222
168 - 109	818 - 629	97 - 28	39 - 18	983 - 444	847 - 561	237 - 168	771 - 378	142 - 118	508 - 299

Four-Digit Numbers With Regrouping

2263 - 1149	3984 - 2267	8590 - 4265	1744 - 1325	6390 - 2125
4582 - 1468	5033 - 2625	7293 - 3184	6188 - 3069	8442 - 1329
9823 - 8216	5436 - 1827	2356 - 2137	7145 - 3829	3961 - 2747
4623 - 3219	1548 - 1239	3892 - 2148	8586 - 2939	5391 - 1872
3879 - 2290	2941 - 1437	6540 - 4019	4258 - 2147	8765 - 2328

Real-life Problem Solving

1 Joshua has 16 video games. He sold eight to a friend, how many video games will Joshua have left?

6 Jacob invited 12 friends to his party. Eight friends attended Jacob's party. How many of the friends he invited did not attend Jacob's party?

2 Emily and nine other girls went out to dinner. Six girls ordered pizza. The other girls ordered cheeseburgers. How many ordered cheeseburgers?

7 Twelve skateboarders entered the skateboarding competition. Five skateboarders attend the same school. How many skateboarders attend other schools?

3 Eleven boys and 14 girls visited the science museum. How many more girls than boys visited the science museum?

8 Tiffany and her mother bought 8 pairs of jeans at the mall. They returned four pairs of jeans to the mall. How many jeans did Tiffany and her mother keep?

4 The company hired 18 new employees. Nine new employees are women. How many new employees are men?

9 Sam's baseball team won 18 games this season. They lost 7 games. How many more games did Sam's team win than it lost?

5 Scientists predict 17 tropical storms this season. The scientists also predict that 8 of these tropical storms will develop into hurricanes. How many tropical storms are not expected to develop into hurricanes?

10 Last year, there were fourteen 1st, 2nd, and 3rd grade classes. This year, there are eleven 1st, 2nd, and 3rd grade classes. How many fewer 1st, 2nd, and 3rd grade classes are there this year?

67

Real-life Problem Solving

1 89 1st and 2nd graders attend Miller School. There are 43 total 2nd graders. How many 1st graders attend Miller School?

6 63 homemade robots were entered into the competition last weekend. 42 robots were destroyed during the competition. How many robots were not destroyed?

2 Rachael and Ryan together read 98 books this school year. Rachel read 51 books. How many books did Ryan read?

7 A total of 24 students auditioned for the school play. Only 14 students were given speaking roles. The others were given nonspeaking roles. How many students were given nonspeaking roles?

3 Yesterday, the 78 4th grade students had their choice of participating in outdoor field games or remaining indoors for gym activities. 42 students remained indoors. How many students went outside for field games?

8 At the grocery store, Todd counted 72 different kinds of cereal. Of these, 39 boxes were priced more than $4.00 per box. How many were priced less than $4.00 per box.

4 The choir has 56 members. There are 14 fewer members in the orchestra. How many members are in the orchestra?

9 Kirsten's family is planning a 95-mile bike ride this weekend. They plan to ride 54 miles on Saturday. How many miles do they plan to ride on Sunday?

5 Both soccer and basketball registration was last week. A total of 83 boys and girls registered. There were 37 who registered for basketball. How many registered for soccer?

10 At the concert, 58 cars were parked in Parking Lot A and 37 cars were parked in Parking Lot B. How many fewer cars were parked in Parking Lot B?

Real-life Problem Solving

1 The video store has 454 total DVDs and VHS tapes of "The Best Movie Ever" for sale. The store has 389 DVDs available. How many VHS tapes are available?

2 At the zoo, one giant sea turtle weighs 476 pounds. Its mate weighs 79 pounds less. What does the sea turtle's mate weigh?

3 At the last swim meet, 129 boys and 118 girls competed. How many more boys competed than girls?

4 In two days, Michael's family drove 894 miles to the shore. The first day they drove 656 miles. How many miles did they drive on the second day?

5 There are 458 new and used cars for sale at the car dealership. This includes 276 used cars. How many new cars are for sale at the car dealership?

6 A total of 342 adults voted in the election for president of the organization. Mr. Keith won the election with 175 votes. How many total votes did the other candidates receive?

7 Christopher works at a popular video game store. On the first day the newest gaming system was released the store sold 493 units. The store sold 118 fewer units on the second day. How many units did the store sell on the second day?

8 Over three days, 844 kids came to the grand opening of the skateboard park. On the first two days, 623 kids came to the park. How many kids came to the park on the third day?

9 Kyle's family has 296 DVDs in its collection. Amanda's family has 348 DVDs in its collection. How many fewer DVDs does Kyle's family have in its collection?

10 Brooke rode her bike 238 miles this summer. Jennifer rode her bike 52 miles less than Brooke. How many miles did Jennifer ride her bike this summer?

Real-life Problem Solving

1 The shopping mall has 933 parking places in its front lot and 848 parking places in its back lot. How many fewer parking places are in the back lot compared to the front lot?

6 Amanda and her brother, Michael, competed in their own video game tournament. Together they played the same racing game 50 times. Michael came in first place 24 times. How many times did Amanda come in first place?

2 Each day 688 students attend Lincoln School. Of those students, 293 ride the school busses. How many students do not ride the school busses each day?

7 Kyle sold 18 candy bars on the first day of the fundraiser. Chad sold 36 candy bars on the first day. How many more candy bars did Chad sell than Kyle on the first day?

3 The school photographer took 375 digital photographs of the championship football game. For the school yearbook only 63 photographs of that game were used. How many photographs were not used?

8 Emily and Rachel enjoyed a day at the amusement park. The amusement park advertises 128 different rides. Emily and Rachel together were able to ride only 73 rides that day. How many rides were they unable to ride?

4 Matthew's family drove 894 miles to Los Angeles, California. James' family drove 743 miles to Las Vegas. How many more miles did Matthew's family drive compared to James' family?

9 Austin had collected 424 miniature die-cast cars. He sold 218 cars in an online auction. How many die-cast cars remain in Austin's collection?

5 The librarian sold 74 books on the first day of the book fair. On the second day, the librarian sold 97 books. How many more books did the librarian sell on the second day compared to the first day?

10 Todd's family owns 129 DVDs and 537 VHS tapes. How many more videotapes than DVDs does the family have?

Name: _____   **Time:** _____   **Correct:** _____ **/100**

1	2	5	3	3	3	4	4	4	5
- 1	- 1	- 2	- 1	- 2	- 3	- 1	- 3	- 0	- 4

5	3	5	4	5	2	2	4	1	3
- 1	- 2	- 3	- 4	- 5	- 2	- 1	- 3	- 1	- 1

5	4	5	3	2	3	5	2	4	5
- 5	- 2	- 0	- 3	- 1	- 2	- 4	- 2	- 3	- 0

2	4	5	3	2	3	5	2	5	3
- 2	- 1	- 5	- 2	- 1	- 0	- 3	- 1	- 4	- 3

1	2	4	3	2	5	4	3	4	5
- 1	- 0	- 2	- 1	- 2	- 2	- 4	- 2	- 3	- 5

2	5	3	4	3	4	5	4	5	4
- 2	- 1	- 2	- 1	- 2	- 3	- 1	- 3	- 2	- 4

5	3	5	4	5	2	2	4	1	3
- 1	- 2	- 3	- 4	- 5	- 2	- 1	- 3	- 1	- 1

5	2	4	3	2	3	5	2	4	5
- 5	- 2	- 1	- 3	- 1	- 2	- 4	- 2	- 3	- 3

1	4	5	3	2	3	5	2	5	3
- 0	- 1	- 5	- 2	- 1	- 0	- 3	- 0	- 4	- 3

1	2	4	3	2	5	5	3	4	5
- 1	- 2	- 0	- 1	- 2	- 2	- 5	- 2	- 3	- 5

Name: **Time:** **Correct:** **/100**

7	10	6	9	7	6	8	6	9	8
- 0	- 1	- 6	- 3	- 4	- 5	- 6	- 0	- 7	- 2
7	6	6	7	10	6	7	9	6	7
- 6	- 1	- 2	- 3	- 4	- 5	- 4	- 0	- 1	- 2
10	9	6	7	8	6	6	9	7	10
- 5	- 4	- 1	- 7	- 5	- 2	- 6	- 3	- 6	- 3
8	6	10	8	9	8	9	7	9	8
- 5	- 2	- 1	- 3	- 6	- 8	- 4	- 7	- 8	- 0
9	9	8	9	8	10	8	7	8	9
- 1	- 7	- 6	- 2	- 5	- 0	- 4	- 3	- 8	- 9
8	10	9	8	6	8	9	10	9	9
- 3	- 6	- 2	- 3	- 4	- 5	- 1	- 7	- 5	- 8
9	10	7	10	7	10	8	10	9	6
- 5	- 2	- 1	- 3	- 6	- 8	- 4	- 7	- 8	- 0
9	8	6	7	10	8	6	8	10	10
- 9	- 7	- 6	- 2	- 5	- 0	- 4	- 3	- 8	- 10
7	7	10	9	9	8	10	8	6	9
- 3	- 6	- 2	- 3	- 9	- 5	- 1	- 7	- 5	- 8
8	9	10	8	8	8	7	8	9	8
- 5	- 2	- 1	- 3	- 6	- 8	- 4	- 7	- 8	- 0

Name: **Time:**   **Correct:**   **/100**

10	12	11	15	12	10	12	13	14	15
- 5	- 2	- 1	- 3	- 10	- 10	- 4	- 7	- 8	- 0

14	14	13	10	11	15	12	14	10	14
- 9	- 7	- 6	- 2	- 10	- 8	- 4	- 3	- 8	- 11

12	15	14	12	11	13	10	15	11	12
- 3	- 13	- 7	- 3	- 9	- 11	- 8	- 7	- 5	- 8

13	13	12	14	15	13	15	14	11	15
- 7	- 8	- 9	- 10	- 12	- 5	- 13	- 7	- 9	- 0

12	10	14	11	14	13	13	15	10	14
- 9	- 7	- 6	- 2	- 5	- 0	- 4	- 3	- 8	- 12

12	15	13	15	12	14	11	14	15	13
- 3	- 10	- 8	- 3	- 9	- 12	- 9	- 7	- 6	- 4

15	13	12	11	13	12	15	12	14	13
- 14	- 6	- 12	- 6	- 9	- 10	- 11	- 9	- 10	- 3

14	15	10	11	14	15	14	14	15	14
- 7	- 8	- 9	- 10	- 11	- 14	- 13	- 8	- 9	- 0

11	12	14	10	11	14	15	12	10	15
- 9	- 7	- 6	- 2	- 5	- 0	- 4	- 3	- 8	- 14

13	12	10	14	12	14	11	16	15	14
- 3	- 10	- 8	- 13	- 9	- 14	- 1	- 7	- 5	- 4

| Name: | | | | Time: | | Correct: | | /100 |

16 - 4	18 - 12	15 - 6	17 - 14	15 - 8	18 - 9	18 - 10	17 - 11	16 - 8	15 - 13
17 - 4	15 - 5	18 - 16	16 - 9	15 - 8	16 - 7	17 - 11	15 - 12	18 - 9	15 - 7
18 - 14	18 - 5	16 - 6	18 - 8	15 - 13	18 - 0	17 - 4	18 - 13	16 - 5	15 - 15
17 - 9	16 - 4	18 - 6	15 - 13	18 - 7	16 - 2	15 - 11	18 - 7	17 - 9	17 - 4
16 - 11	15 - 2	15 - 14	18 - 12	16 - 14	18 - 10	17 - 0	18 - 9	16 - 9	18 - 18
17 - 4	16 - 8	16 - 12	15 - 9	18 - 8	17 - 9	18 - 10	15 - 12	16 - 7	17 - 13
16 - 14	15 - 14	18 - 17	15 - 2	17 - 5	15 - 10	17 - 14	16 - 3	17 - 10	18 - 15
17 - 13	18 - 11	16 - 4	15 - 13	18 - 9	16 - 15	15 - 1	16 - 0	17 - 3	18 - 2
15 - 1	16 - 16	18 - 15	15 - 6	18 - 9	17 - 2	16 - 11	17 - 8	15 - 10	17 - 13
18 - 13	15 - 10	16 - 2	15 - 9	18 - 7	15 - 12	17 - 9	18 - 2	16 - 9	15 - 14

Name: **Time:**   **Correct:**   **/100**

10 − 2	9 − 2	18 − 4	9 − 5	11 − 9	7 − 6	8 − 6	9 − 6	10 − 7	5 − 5
18 − 2	6 − 5	7 − 4	10 − 8	12 − 7	6 − 3	10 − 9	14 − 7	5 − 5	17 − 9
16 − 1	4 − 3	5 − 4	18 − 16	8 − 5	17 − 7	12 − 4	10 − 3	11 − 7	3 − 3
9 − 9	6 − 5	11 − 7	14 − 8	9 − 2	16 − 7	8 − 2	10 − 3	16 − 2	12 − 11
6 − 1	17 − 13	18 − 12	9 − 9	2 − 1	6 − 5	7 − 2	9 − 7	10 − 3	5 − 3
3 − 2	4 − 3	11 − 8	10 − 6	8 − 5	5 − 5	10 − 7	8 − 1	6 − 2	9 − 8
14 − 2	3 − 3	17 − 9	9 − 1	16 − 3	9 − 8	10 − 8	11 − 3	9 − 6	6 − 3
10 − 1	6 − 6	8 − 4	10 − 7	10 − 6	4 − 4	10 − 8	16 − 0	1 − 1	17 − 5
16 − 4	10 − 9	9 − 3	10 − 7	8 − 2	11 − 4	10 − 9	9 − 3	14 − 8	8 − 7
17 − 7	8 − 3	9 − 5	18 − 12	10 − 4	16 − 4	7 − 6	10 − 3	12 − 8	8 − 6

Name: **Time:**   **Correct:**   **/100**

18 − 2	17 − 2	18 − 4	12 − 5	14 − 9	9 − 6	6 − 6	9 − 8	7 − 7	8 − 5
14 − 12	15 − 7	17 − 13	8 − 8	13 − 6	16 − 3	11 − 9	12 − 7	15 − 5	16 − 8
13 − 9	5 − 3	12 − 4	16 − 16	6 − 5	18 − 7	12 − 4	10 − 7	11 − 3	8 − 3
10 − 9	12 − 5	14 − 7	15 − 8	8 − 2	15 − 7	12 − 2	11 − 3	7 − 2	11 − 11
16 − 14	14 − 13	18 − 8	10 − 9	12 − 11	7 − 5	9 − 1	8 − 6	12 − 3	5 − 2
11 − 2	14 − 5	12 − 6	7 − 6	9 − 6	11 − 4	13 − 8	8 − 7	3 − 2	9 − 2
13 − 2	10 − 6	11 − 2	9 − 8	8 − 3	12 − 4	17 − 9	16 − 13	8 − 2	11 − 3
9 − 1	7 − 7	12 − 6	18 − 4	11 − 7	13 − 6	4 − 4	10 − 8	9 − 3	6 − 5
15 − 14	11 − 4	9 − 1	7 − 7	12 − 12	11 − 8	9 − 8	9 − 3	13 − 5	1 − 0
17 − 0	8 − 3	12 − 7	18 − 12	14 − 14	16 − 4	7 − 6	10 − 0	17 − 8	18 − 9

Name: **Time:**   **Correct:**   **/100**

18	14	12	11	8	10	7	18	14	13
- 9	- 4	- 3	- 6	- 1	- 0	- 6	- 7	- 7	- 5

13	11	12	9	6	4	3	9	10	15
- 2	- 4	- 6	- 1	- 2	- 2	- 3	- 2	- 4	- 7

14	8	15	13	12	18	12	16	18	7
- 11	- 6	- 4	- 7	- 2	- 15	- 9	- 8	- 13	- 4

10	12	14	15	8	15	12	11	7	12
- 9	- 5	- 7	- 8	- 2	- 7	- 2	- 3	- 2	- 10

12	17	5	8	13	6	10	14	11	5
- 11	- 2	- 4	- 5	- 11	- 1	- 9	- 8	- 2	- 4

13	10	17	9	13	11	13	5	14	8
- 10	- 3	- 8	- 2	- 4	- 2	- 8	- 3	- 12	- 6

18	6	7	9	18	16	14	12	1	5
- 2	- 6	- 4	- 7	- 13	- 11	- 4	- 5	- 1	- 2

18	12	11	16	16	14	13	8	10	7
- 2	- 4	- 8	- 12	- 7	- 5	- 9	- 2	- 7	- 1

14	13	10	8	3	5	18	16	14	11
- 14	- 4	- 8	- 8	- 2	- 4	- 8	- 16	- 5	- 10

12	9	13	17	13	15	17	11	18	17
- 4	- 3	- 7	- 13	- 12	- 14	- 6	- 9	- 8	- 8

Name: **Time:**   **Correct:**   **/50**

35 - 23	72 - 30	87 - 13	66 - 32	75 - 14	62 - 32	30 - 10	47 - 21	71 - 11	58 - 18
54 - 12	39 - 19	46 - 16	64 - 34	66 - 26	58 - 12	67 - 57	98 - 62	42 - 22	31 - 31
76 - 33	86 - 24	95 - 21	57 - 21	45 - 31	59 - 13	87 - 72	91 - 80	32 - 12	22 - 11
46 - 22	28 - 13	94 - 23	61 - 40	99 - 33	44 -42	32 - 21	69 - 58	54 - 23	38 - 26
27 - 16	46 - 24	91 - 11	68 - 46	59 - 52	22 - 12	27 - 26	48 - 27	59 - 14	43 - 23

51 − 23	65 − 36	82 − 23	63 − 34	81 − 46	55 − 28	28 − 19	48 − 39	31 − 14	77 − 18
63 − 19	47 − 18	41 − 26	73 − 39	58 − 29	63 − 18	44 − 39	57 − 38	61 − 28	27 − 18
53 − 44	36 − 18	42 − 26	65 − 46	71 − 32	68 − 19	51 − 23	35 − 27	28 − 19	95 − 66
76 − 27	41 − 18	93 − 26	56 − 17	82 − 33	24 − 18	37 − 28	44 − 35	51 − 34	91 − 86
85 − 28	71 − 25	64 − 15	57 − 28	32 − 14	73 − 18	92 − 27	74 − 68	36 − 17	58 − 29

Name:		Time:	Correct:	/25

672 - 258	587 - 543	451 - 189	853 - 348	658 - 487
787 - 439	742 - 578	259 - 259	657 - 387	825 - 729
403 - 136	537 - 325	682 - 386	143 - 103	502 - 291
561 - 437	119 - 102	215 - 163	783 - 541	102 - 100
317 - 165	602 - 539	741 - 528	361 - 218	317 - 209

| Name: | | Time: | | Correct: | | /50 |

10	9	6	7	8	6	6	9	7	10
- 5	- 4	- 1	- 7	- 5	- 2	- 6	- 3	- 6	- 3

53	36	42	65	71	68	54	35	28	95
- 44	- 18	- 26	- 46	- 32	- 19	- 23	- 27	- 19	- 66

13	8	10	17	9	13	11	5	14	8
- 10	- 7	- 3	- 8	- 2	- 4	- 2	- 3	- 12	- 6

317	602	741	361	317
- 165	- 539	- 328	- 218	- 209

86	73	96	68	55	33	27	58	69	29
- 63	- 50	- 45	- 17	- 14	- 21	- 16	- 42	- 33	- 16

787	742	983	657	825
- 439	- 578	- 547	- 387	- 729

47	53	77	73	62	58	27	87	98	31
- 28	- 25	- 38	- 46	- 18	- 39	- 19	- 19	- 73	- 25

214	305	272	143	502
- 136	- 236	- 168	- 103	- 468

10	12	14	15	8	15	12	11	7	12
- 9	- 5	- 7	- 8	- 5	- 7	- 2	- 3	- 2	- 10

672	587	451	853	658
- 258	- 543	- 189	- 348	- 487

76	41	93	56	82	24	37	44	51	91
- 27	- 18	- 26	- 17	- 33	- 18	- 28	- 35	- 34	- 86

14	8	15	13	12	7	18	12	16	18
- 11	- 6	- 4	- 7	- 2	- 4	- 15	- 9	- 8	- 13

Name:		Time:		Correct:		/50

621	781	669	863	587
- 427	- 514	- 485	- 383	- 194

11	9	12	15	6	15	10	11	18	18
- 9	- 5	- 7	- 12	- 2	- 8	- 2	- 3	- 2	- 10

554	914	778	358	851
- 328	- 345	- 498	- 176	- 784

67	94	39	65	77	42	63	87	64	89
- 58	- 81	- 29	- 23	- 49	- 19	- 54	- 38	- 35	- 27

33	11	15	9	18	11	14	17	65	39
- 17	- 2	- 4	- 7	- 16	- 9	- 5	- 7	- 26	- 28

74	62	58	21	59	64	98	81	73	55
- 37	- 24	- 29	- 14	- 32	- 38	- 49	- 55	- 16	- 26

Name:	Time:	Correct:	/50

32	35	88	69	42	65	78	62	98	36
- 28	- 15	- 83	- 22	- 11	- 26	- 52	- 58	- 29	- 27

421	893	521	698	504
- 227	- 432	- 118	- 465	- 373

8	3	12	18	5	17	12	11	10	9
- 2	- 2	- 4	- 5	- 2	- 5	- 6	- 6	- 5	- 2

452	906	704	717	365
- 384	- 176	- 528	- 422	- 218

76	54	38	57	45	59	87	91	32	22
- 33	- 37	- 22	- 21	- 31	- 13	- 72	- 80	- 12	- 11

17	8	5	9	11	7	9	12	11	14
- 12	- 3	- 1	- 2	- 4	- 4	- 0	- 3	- 6	- 6

Name: **Time:**   **Correct:**   **/50**

832	605	397	822	346
- 550	- 329	- 63	- 211	- 187

12	17	5	8	13	6	10	14	11	5
- 11	- 2	- 4	- 5	- 11	- 1	- 9	- 8	- 2	- 4

561	875	357	407	219
- 414	- 824	- 29	- 144	- 169

35	72	87	66	75	62	30	47	71	58
- 23	- 30	- 13	- 32	- 14	- 32	- 10	- 21	- 11	- 18

8	9	11	12	19	2	7	15	9	8
- 3	- 2	- 9	- 7	- 9	- 1	- 5	- 9	- 6	- 7

55	39	87	49	63	29	17	99	37	88
- 21	- 25	- 37	- 46	- 53	- 18	- 17	- 87	- 17	- 23

Name: **Time:**   **Correct:**   **/50**

60 - 14	57 - 38	83 - 18	88 - 69	55 - 37	68 - 59	71 - 36	92 - 14	26 - 17	80 - 64

682 - 291	581 - 403	523 - 312	685 - 527	347 - 129

14 - 14	13 - 2	10 - 8	8 - 8	3 - 2	5 - 4	18 - 8	16 - 16	14 - 5	11 - 10

561 - 238	875 - 738	357 - 149	407 - 122	209 - 149

54 - 12	39 - 19	46 - 16	64 - 34	66 - 26	58 - 12	67 - 57	98 - 62	42 - 22	31 - 31

10 - 9	12 - 5	14 - 7	15 - 8	8 - 2	15 - 7	12 - 2	11 - 3	7 - 2	11 - 11

Name: **Time:**   **Correct:**   **/50**

37	43	61	80	78	35	92	73	38	46
- 18	- 24	- 22	- 41	- 19	- 26	- 64	- 55	- 19	- 27

65	21	58	48	70	49	78	84	65	83
- 14	- 18	- 31	- 21	- 45	- 14	- 24	- 38	- 44	- 22

12	8	10	17	9	13	11	5	14	8
- 10	- 7	- 3	- 8	- 2	- 4	- 2	- 3	- 12	- 6

15	13	17	12	18	14	11	12	8	7
- 12	- 4	- 8	- 4	- 6	- 9	- 3	- 9	- 2	- 4

11	8	7	18	11	12	14	11	18	16
- 11	- 4	- 4	- 14	- 3	- 11	- 3	- 5	- 12	- 14

CLAIM THAT NUMBER

Your understanding of Fact Families will help you in this challenging card game. You can play this game alone or with one or more friends. Cut out the cards on pages 89-91. To play, shuffle the cards and place five cards face up on the table. Place the rest of the deck face down and turn over the top card. The number on this card is the number to be claimed.

Try to claim the number on the top card by adding or subtracting any two of the five face-up cards. If you're successful, take all three cards. Draw two more cards and place them face up in the center, and turn the top card over to be claimed. If you're unable to claim the top card, simply turn over another top card. If you're playing with a friend, take turns and the player who has claimed the most cards at the end wins

The number to be named is 6. It may be named with 4+2, 8-2, or 10-4.
If you choose 4+2, take the 4, 2, and 6 cards

The new number to be claimed is 15. This number cannot be claimed.
Turn over the next card from the face-down deck and place it on top of 15.
This is the new number to be claimed. If you're playing with friends,
it becomes the next player's turn.

For more challenging play, use any combination of cards to claim the number.
For example, 7 + 7 + 1 = 16   If the game is too difficult, increase the number of face-up cards.